These primers on Jon  passion for God—pro
unto God. And they l
majesty of our Savior. ....
Douglas Sweeney for making Edwards and his vision of God so
accessible to the rest of us thirsty pilgrims.

>—**Thabiti Anyabwile**, Pastor of First Baptist Church of
> Grand Cayman, Cayman Islands

Everyone says Jonathan Edwards is important. Quite frankly,
however, his writing style is pretty dense by contemporary standards, so few pastors and other Christian leaders have invested
much time reading him. This new series tackles the problem.
Here is the kernel of much of Edwards's thought in eminently
accessible form.

>—**D. A. Carson**, Research Professor of New Testament,
> Trinity Evangelical Divinity School

In *The Essential Edwards Collection*, Owen Strachan and Doug
Sweeney point with knowledge and excitement to clear and
searching sections that illuminate God's truth and search our
hearts. In this collection, Edwards is introduced to a new generation of readers. His concerns are made our concerns. This is a
worthy effort and I pray that God will bless it.

>—**Mark Dever**, Senior Pastor, Capitol Hill Baptist
> Church, Washington, DC

I am deeply impressed with the vision that has brought together
this splendid library of volumes to introduce Jonathan Edwards to
a new generation. Owen Strachan and Douglas Sweeney have
provided an incredible service by making the often challenging
writings of America's greatest theologian accessible for seasoned
theologians, pastors, and students alike with their five-volume
Essential Edwards Collection. This series is properly titled the
"essential collection."

>—**David S. Dockery**, President, Union University

This series is a fantastic introduction to the heart, mind, and ministry of the greatest theologian America has ever produced.

—**Mark Driscoll**, Pastor of Mars Hill Church, President of the Acts 29 Church Planting Network

Jonathan Edwards was a preacher of the Word, a pastor of souls, a philosopher of first rank, and the greatest theologian America has ever produced. In this wonderful new anthology of Edwards's writings, the great Puritan saint lives again. I can think of no better tonic for our transcendence-starved age than the writings of Edwards. But beware: reading this stuff can change your life forever!

—**Timothy George**, Founding Dean of Beeson Divinity School of Samford University

Let Strachan and Sweeney serve as your guides through the voluminous writings of America's greatest theologian. They have been shaped by his godly counsel and moved by his passion for Christ. By God's grace, Edwards can do the same for you. Start your journey with *The Essential Edwards Collection.*

—**Collin Hansen**, Author of *Young, Restless, Reformed*

Owen Strachan and Douglas Sweeney have done us all a great service by remixing and reloading the teaching of Jonathan Edwards for a new generation. They do more than introduce us to his writing: they show us how his biblical teaching relates to a modern world and leave us hungry for more. I am very impressed and very grateful for *The Essential Edwards Collection.*

—**Joshua Harris**, Senior Pastor of Covenant Life Church

From a course he taught at Yale and in personal friendship, Doug Sweeney has taught me much about Edwards. Possessing a command of the academic field, he and Owen Strachan nevertheless write this collection with pastoral concern, showing the relevance of Edwards for our Christian faith and practice today. It's a rare combination of gifts and insights that Sweeney and Strachan bring to this task.

> —**Michael Horton**, J. Gresham Machen Professor of Systematic Theology and Apologetics, Westminster Theological Seminary California

When it comes to Jonathan Edwards's writing, where does an average reader (like me!) begin? Right here, with *The Essential Edwards Collection*. Strachan and Sweeney provide a doorway into the life and teaching of one of the church's wisest theologians. The authors have also included notes of personal application to help us apply the life and teaching of Edwards to our own lives. I've read no better introduction to Jonathan Edwards.

> —**C. J. Mahaney**, President of Sovereign Grace Ministries

Why hasn't this been done before? *The Essential Edwards Collection* is now essential reading for the serious-minded Christian. Doug Sweeney and Owen Strachan have written five excellent and accessible introductions to America's towering theological genius—Jonathan Edwards. They combine serious scholarship with the ability to make Edwards and his theology come alive for a new generation. *The Essential Edwards Collection* is a great achievement and a tremendous resource. I can't think of a better way to gain a foundational knowledge of Edwards and his lasting significance.

> —**R. Albert Mohler Jr.**, President of The Southern Baptist Theological Seminary

A great resource! Edwards continues to speak, and this series of books is an excellent means to hear Jonathan Edwards again live and clear. Pure gold; be wise and invest in it!

> —**Dr. Josh Moody**, Senior Pastor, College Church in Wheaton.

You hold in your hands a unique resource: a window into the life and thought of Jonathan Edwards, a man whose life was captured by God for the gospel of Jesus Christ. In these pages you'll not only learn about Edwards, but you'll be able to hear him speak in his own words. This winsome and accessible introduction is now the first thing I'd recommend for those who want to know more about America's greatest pastor-theologian.

—**Justin Taylor**, Managing Editor, ESV Study Bible

Jonathan Edwards is surely one of the most influential theologians of the eighteenth century. Now, at last, we have a wide-ranging and representative sample of his work published in an attractive, accessible and, most important of all, readable form. The authors are to be commended for the work they have put into this set and I hope it will become an important feature of the library of many pastors and students of the Christian faith.

—**Carl R. Trueman**, Academic Dean, Westminster Theological Seminary

JONATHAN EDWARDS
on THE GOOD LIFE

THE ESSENTIAL
EDWARDS
COLLECTION

OWEN STRACHAN *and* DOUGLAS SWEENEY

MOODY PUBLISHERS
CHICAGO

© 2010 by
OWEN STRACHAN
DOUGLAS SWEENEY

All websites listed herein are accurate at the time of publication, but may change in
the future or cease to exist. The listing of website references and resources does not
imply publisher endorsement of the site's entire contents. Groups, corporations, and
organizations are listed for informational purposes, and listing does not imply publisher endorsement of their activities.

Editor: Christopher Reese
Interior Design: Ragont Design
Cover Design: Gearbox

Library of Congress Cataloging-in-Publication Data

Strachan, Owen.
    Jonathan Edwards on the good life / Owen Strachan and Douglas Sweeney.
    p. cm. — (The essential Edwards collection)
    Includes bibliographical references.
    ISBN 978-0-8024-2459-4
    1. Edwards, Jonathan, 1703-1758. 2. Christian life. I. Sweeney, Douglas A.
II. Title.
BV4501.3.S773 2009
248.4—dc22

                                                                    2009040814

We hope you enjoy this book from Moody Publishers. Our goal is to provide high-
quality, thought-provoking books and products that connect truth to your real needs
and challenges. For more information on other books and products written and produced from a biblical perspective, go to www.moodypublishers.com or write to:

Moody Publishers
820 N. LaSalle Boulevard
Chicago, IL 60610

1 3 5 7 9 10 8 6 4 2

Printed in the United States of America

The Essential Edwards Collection

Jonathan Edwards: Lover of God

Jonathan Edwards on Beauty

Jonathan Edwards on Heaven and Hell

Jonathan Edwards on the Good Life

Jonathan Edwards on True Christianity

OS

To Keegan,
whom God used to show me
what the good life truly is

DS

To Wilma Sweeney,
who has helped me
understand and live the good life

CONTENTS

Abbreviations of Works Cited

The following shortened forms of books by or about Jonathan Edwards are used in the text to indicate the source of quotations.

Kimnach, Wilson H., Kenneth P. Minkema, and Douglas A. Sweeney, eds. *The Sermons of Jonathan Edwards: A Reader.* New Haven: Yale Univ. Press, 1999.
Cited as "Kimnach" in the text.

Books in the Yale University Press *Works of Jonathan Edwards* series

In the text, the volumes are listed in the following format: (*Works* 1, 200). The "1" refers to the series volume; the "200" refers to the page number in the given volume.

Edwards, Jonathan. *Religious Affections*, ed. John Smith, *The Works of Jonathan Edwards*, vol. 2. New Haven: Yale, 1959.

_____. *Original Sin*, ed. Clyde A. Holbrook, *The Works of Jonathan Edwards*, vol. 3. New Haven: Yale, 1970.

_____. *Ethical Writings*, ed. Paul Ramsay, *The Works of Jonathan Edwards*, vol. 8. New Haven: Yale, 1989.

_____. *Sermons and Discourses, 1723–1729*, ed. Kenneth E. Minkema, *The Works of Jonathan Edwards*, vol. 14. New Haven: Yale, 1997.

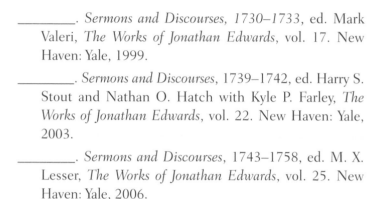

_____. *Sermons and Discourses, 1730–1733*, ed. Mark Valeri, *The Works of Jonathan Edwards*, vol. 17. New Haven: Yale, 1999.

_____. *Sermons and Discourses*, 1739–1742, ed. Harry S. Stout and Nathan O. Hatch with Kyle P. Farley, *The Works of Jonathan Edwards*, vol. 22. New Haven: Yale, 2003.

_____. *Sermons and Discourses*, 1743–1758, ed. M. X. Lesser, *The Works of Jonathan Edwards*, vol. 25. New Haven: Yale, 2006.

Jonathan Edwards, a God-Entranced Man

*W*hen I was in seminary, a wise professor told me that besides the Bible I should choose one great theologian and apply myself throughout life to understanding and mastering his thought. This way I would sink at least one shaft deep into reality, rather than always dabbling on the surface of things. I might come to know at least one system with which to bring other ideas into fruitful dialogue. It was good advice.

The theologian I have devoted myself to is Jonathan Edwards. All I knew of Edwards when I went to seminary was that he preached a sermon called "Sinners in the Hands of an Angry God," in which he said something about hanging over hell by a slender thread. My first real encounter with Edwards was when I read his "Essay on the Trinity" and wrote a paper on it for church history.

It had a lasting effect on me. It gave me a conceptual framework with which to grasp, in part, the meaning of saying God is three in one. In brief, there is God the Father, the fountain of being, who from all eternity has had a perfectly clear and distinct image and idea of himself; and this image is the eternally begotten Son. Between this Son and Father there flows a stream of infinitely vigorous love and perfectly holy communion; and this is God the Spirit. God's Image of God and God's Love of God are so full of God that they are fully divine Persons, and not less.

After graduation from college, and before my wife and I took off for graduate work in Germany, we spent some restful days on a small farm in Barnesville, Georgia. Here I had another encounter with Edwards. Sitting on one of those old-fashioned two-seater swings in the backyard under a big hickory tree, with pen in hand, I read *The Nature of True Virtue.* I have a long entry in my journal from July 14, 1971, in which I try to understand, with Edwards's help, why a Christian is obligated to forgive wrongs when there seems to be a moral law in our hearts that cries out against evil in the world.

Later, when I was in my doctoral program in Germany, I encountered Edwards's *Dissertation Concerning the End for Which God Created the World.* I read it in a pantry in our little apartment in Munich. The pantry was about 8 by 5 feet, a most unlikely place to read a book like the Dissertation. From my perspective now, I would say that if there were one book that captures the essence or wellspring of Edwards's theology, this would be it. Edwards's answer to the question of why God created the world is this: to emanate the fullness of His glory for His people to know, praise, and enjoy. Here is the heart of his theology in his own words:

> IT APPEARS THAT ALL that is ever spoken of in the Scrip-ture as an ultimate end of God's works is included in that one phrase, *the glory of God.* In the creatures' knowing, esteeming, loving, rejoicing in and praising God, the glory of God is both exhibited and acknowledged; his fullness is received and returned. Here is both the *emanation* and *rem-anation.* The refulgence shines upon and into the creature, and is reflected back to the luminary. The beams of glory come from God, and are something of God and are refunded back again to their original. So that the whole is *of* God and *in* God, and *to* God, and God is the beginning, middle and end in this affair. (*Works* 8, 531)

That is the heart and center of Jonathan Edwards and, I believe, of the Bible too. That kind of reading can turn a pantry into a vestibule of heaven.

I am not the only person for whom Edwards continues to be a vestibule of heaven. I hear testimonies regularly that people have stumbled upon this man's work and had their world turned upside down. There are simply not many writers today whose mind and heart are God-entranced the way Edwards was. Again and again, to this very day his writings help me know that experience.

My prayer for *The Essential Edwards Collection* is that it will draw more people into the sway of Edwards's God-entranced worldview. I hope that many who start here, or continue here, will make their way to Edwards himself. Amazingly, almost everything he wrote is available on the Internet. And increasingly his works are available in affordable books. I am thankful that Owen Strachan and Douglas Sweeney share my conviction that every effort to point to Edwards, and through him to his God, is a worthy investment of our lives. May that be the outcome of these volumes.

John Piper
Pastor for Preaching and Vision
Bethlehem Baptist Church
Minneapolis, Minnesota

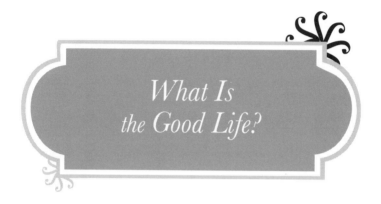

*What Is
the Good Life?*

*W*hen you think about the "good life," what comes to
    mind?

Is it cars that drive fast or houses that resemble castles?

Is it unrestrained gratification of all one's desires or
unbounded sexual pleasure?

Relentless activism and social involvement or being swal-
lowed up in an earthly cause that promises some form of
utopian progress?

Or is it obedient Christian faith, birthed in the grace of
God, that transforms one's life, one's environment, and one's
eternal destiny?

As one can see, there are a variety of responses to the

answer, and many more not listed here. Modern life, with instantaneous amenities, globalized markets, and a massive economic system promises nothing less than constant and instant satisfaction for all our wants and needs. There seems to be nothing beyond our fingertips, nothing that we cannot get, and thus there is very little reason to restrain ourselves, to rein in our desire for whatever we wish to have.

There is another way of life, however, that is not necessarily disconnected from modern life, but which proceeds from an ancient book that lifts life in this age and all others to another plane. This is the truly good life, the path plotted for mankind by almighty God. It involves sacrifice, and hardship, and hard work. It requires self-denial, self-abasement, and an others-centered mindset. It is radically God-centered and deeply rooted in Scripture. This, and no other path, leads to lasting happiness for the souls of human beings.

It is the purpose of this book to explore the dimensions of the good life. We have for our guide the master theologian and pastor, Jonathan Edwards. Working out of a small parish in eighteenth-century Massachusetts, Edwards created through his body of sermons and theological writings an exhilarating portrait of the life God intended His created race to live. We present this subject matter by interacting with the actual writing of Edwards. It will take a little time to get used to his style, but it is our belief that investing even a little effort in reading his writing will yield a huge spiritual payoff. We will mix in our commentary on his writing even as we sketch a general picture of his views on the good life. As we go, we will offer brief suggestions for application of his views that we hope will be of use to you in your personal reading or in the context of group study.

Though we both enjoy delving deeply into subjects like this one, we cannot cover every base in this book. The broader *Essential Edwards Collection* allows the reader to delve much deeper into his thinking and preaching, but we seek in *Jonathan Edwards on the Good Life* to bring to light a central theme of Edwards's thought, one often overlooked but filled with rich discoveries. We seek to make Edwards accessible to a wide audience. This book is intended for the uninitiated, but we hope and intend for it—and for this series—to be of use to pastors, students, church leaders, small groups, and many more besides.

In the five chapters that follow, we intend to show the original design of God for mankind, the effect of sin upon this design, the transforming effect of conversion, the blessings inherent in the Christian life, and the way God's gracious commandments lead us to the sweetest possible experience of His love. Along the way, we will find fresh faith for our daily lives and discover the true shape of the good life, the existence God has specially designed for our flourishing and our joy.

CHAPTER ONE

The Nearness of the Good Life

The gaze is direct. The posture is straight. The face is serious, even stern. In his portraits, Jonathan Edwards stares back at the viewer. To a person unfamiliar with the theologian, he looks like any other stereotypical colonial parson, severe and austere, brooking no foolishness, itching to declaim the evils of everyday life. Wearing a powdered wig of tight white curls, staring alertly back at the observer, Jonathan Edwards as portrayed on canvas seems to substantiate the image of Edwards cultivated for generations in high-school classrooms. Here is the man who unleashed the thunder of "Sinners in the Hands of an Angry God." Small wonder that such a gloomy person would bore into us from his portrait.

But appearances are often deceiving. In reality, Jonathan Edwards was not an angry man. He was one of the happiest men around. He loved to play and talk with his children, and he enjoyed much cheer and laughter in his marriage to his wife, Sarah. He cherished his time in his study. Jonathan's happiness, however, transcended the joys of home and work, significant as they are. Unlike many people, Jonathan Edwards knew happiness at the very core of his being. In a way that many of us don't even think about, Edwards possessed a holistic intellectual and spiritual happiness. He strove to know God with his mind, to experience the goodness of God with his heart, and to lead others to do the same. Though his temperament was calm, he lived with zest and vigor, modeling the happy way of life he taught his people.

Many people today do not know such peace and happiness. They live with constant tension, often acting contrary to what their mind and their conscience tell them is right. They rebel against their Creator and His design for their life. Though they may know satisfaction for a brief period, lasting happiness evades them. This results in a broken, frustrating, ultimately pointless life.

Though his era differed from ours, Jonathan identified the same problem in his day. Gifted from his youth with great passion for God and His Word, Jonathan discovered early on in his life that true and lasting happiness in this life was attainable. All that the human heart desired it could have, and far more besides. The riches of God's Word could satisfy the intellectual hunger of the human mind for a balanced, cohesive, meaningful worldview and the spiritual hunger of the human heart for a joyful, hopeful, transformative existence.

In sum, Jonathan discovered a simple but vitalizing truth: God had not made mankind to be miserable. Being a Christian did not mean the absence of pleasure. Much to the contrary, God had made mankind to experience unending delight and joy in Him, to be happier and happier as knowledge of God increased, and to constantly soak up the sweetest pleasure the world affords in the life of faith—all of which flow together to constitute "the good life." In a world filled with people who lived in the gloom of darkness, Jonathan Edwards preached to set his hearers' hearts on fire, to alter forever the way they understood themselves and their lives. He knew that any life created by the majestic, undomesticated, loving God of the Bible could not be mundane or boring. He preached in such a way as to altogether change the way we think about our faith and the way we practice it.

In this chapter, we will explore the initial, pre-fall design of God for human life through interaction with a number of noteworthy Edwardsean texts: *The Dissertation Concerning the End for Which God Created the World*, the *Dissertation Concerning the Nature of True Virtue*, the sermon "Charity Contrary to a Selfish Spirit," and the homily "The Pleasantness of Religion." By careful study of these sources, we will develop an understanding of the original intention of the Creator for mankind and clear our minds of false and unbiblical conceptions of the good, Christian life. God, we shall see in this chapter, has not made people to be grimly obedient.

Rather, He desires that we find transcendent, unassailable, undimmed satisfaction in Him.

God the Foundation

The foundation of the good life is God. In Edwards's world, God reigned over all as the emblem of majesty, authority, and goodness. The sum of His perfections rendered God beautiful, or more accurately, Beauty itself. As covered in *Jonathan Edwards on Beauty*, also in this series, God created the world to display and reflect His glory. All that the eye can see exists to "remanate," or send back, God's original glory to Himself. God alone is worthy of such a system, for He alone is God. All of creation participates in this "cycle of beauty" that begins with God and returns to God.

But while all things in some way display and reflect the beauty of God, only humans may do so with awareness. Only mankind can participate consciously in the cycle of beauty. It was for this very purpose that God created the race. He desired a special sort of being to commune with Him and to joyfully image His goodness in the world. Edwards discussed this in his foundational text *The End for Which God Created the World*:

> IT SEEMS TO BE A THING in itself fit and desirable, that the glorious perfections of God should be known, and the operations and expressions of them seen by other beings besides himself. . . . As God's perfections are things in them–

selves excellent, so the expression of them in their proper acts and fruits is excellent, and the knowledge of these excellent perfections, and of these glorious expressions of them, is an excellent thing, the existence of which is in itself valuable and desirable.

Because God was so excellent, it was only right that His excellence be enjoyed by others:

> 'TIS A THING INFINITELY GOOD in itself that God's glory should be known by a glorious society of created beings. And that there should be in them an increasing knowledge of God to all eternity is an existence, a reality infinitely worthy to be, and worthy to be valued and regarded by him, to whom it belongs in order that it be, which, of all things possible, is fittest and best. If existence is more worthy than defect and nonentity, and if any created existence is in itself worthy to be, then knowledge or understanding is a thing worthy to be; and if any knowledge, then the most excellent sort of knowledge, viz. that of God and his glory. The existence of the created universe consists as much in it as in anything: yea, this knowledge is one of the highest, most real and substantial parts, of all created existence most remote from nonentity and defect. (*Works* 8, 430–32)

The passage touches on numerous ideas, but the key sentence
for our purposes is this: "'Tis a thing infinitely good in itself
that God's glory should be known by a glorious society of created beings." Edwards believed that mankind was made for
an "increasing knowledge of God," a knowledge of "the most
excellent sort" that would satisfy and fill the mind and heart
as nothing else can. Adam and Eve, and the race they produced, were not mere chess pawns in the hands of the Grand-
master, but possessed a supremely noble purpose that would
make for a life of the most exhilarating kind.

The Good Life Does Not Squash Happiness

In giving his picture of the good life, Edwards had to overcome two specific objections. First, he had to show how a universe that existed to glorify God did not squash or prohibit the
happiness of mankind. Central to the following passage is the
idea that God "emanates" or sends His beauty (or glory) out,
and the creature receives and delights in it. Edwards teaches
us here that the happiness of God and the happiness of
humanity are not, as some have suggested, at odds. Instead,
God and man ideally work in harmony, with God "emanating"
glory that is received and reflected by mankind, who grows
happy in performing this divine duty:

GOD IN SEEKING HIS GLORY, therein seeks the good of his
creatures: because the emanation of his glory (which he
seeks and delights in, as he delights in himself and his own

eternal glory) implies the communicated excellency and
happiness of his creature. And that in communicating his
fullness for them, he does it for himself: because their good,
which he seeks, is so much in union and communion with
himself. God is their good. Their excellency and happiness
is nothing but the emanation and expression of God's
glory: God in seeking their glory and happiness, seeks himself: and in seeking himself, i.e. himself diffused and
expressed (which he delights in, as he delights in his own
beauty and fullness), he seeks their glory and happiness.

Edwards continued the argument by putting it in grander terms:

IN THIS VIEW IT APPEARS that God's respect to the creature, in the whole, unites with his respect to himself. Both
regards are like two lines which seem at the beginning to
be separate, but aim finally to meet in one, both being
directed to the same center. And as to the good of the creature itself, if viewed in its whole duration, and infinite pro-
gression, it must be viewed as infinite; and so not only
being some communication of God's glory, but as coming
nearer and nearer to the same thing in its infinite fullness.
The nearer anything comes to infinite, the nearer it comes
to an identity with God. And if any good, as viewed by
God, is beheld as infinite, it can't be viewed as a distinct
thing from God's own infinite glory. (*Works* 8, 459)

In this passage, Edwards refutes the charge that God's glory and man's happiness are mutually exclusive. His central point is that "God in seeking his glory, therein seeks the good of his creatures." As some mistakenly believed, if God is going to be happy, then He will create a world that pleases only Himself and that yields little or no happiness to the people placed in the world to do His bidding. Humanity functions as little more than a race of slaves forced to execute the tyrannical will of a cruel king. Edwards, however, shows that this line of thought fails miserably. God, if He is God, is not a tyrant. As God, He is the embodiment of goodness. "[T]he emanation of his glory (which he seeks and delights in, as he delights in himself and his own eternal glory)," then, "implies the communicated excellency and happiness of his creature." Life as this kind and awesome God created it to be cannot be slavish or sad; it is filled with "excellency and happiness" that flows from the divine fountain.

All of the God-centered life is calibrated to bless the people of God as they glorify the Lord in all they do (1 Corinthians 10:31). Those who seek the Lord and live to magnify Him will know His "communicated excellency and happiness" even as they participate in the great work of glorifying Him. God's glory and man's happiness are not at odds with one another—far from it. The two ideally work hand in hand.

Thus we see Edwards's brilliant and transformative doctrine of the good life. At its deepest, most profound level, the good life is the life lived for the glory of God. Those who live to display and image the beauty of God will, in whatever circumstance they find themselves, experience happiness that comes directly from God Himself. Happiness, then, is not a state outside of ourselves that we must strive for. It does not ebb and flow with our life situation. Happiness *is* doing the will of God, for the will of God always yields the glory of God. What is the will of God? It is God's revealed purposes and desires in the Bible. In short, the good life is the existence that takes shape according to the teachings and commands of Scripture. When one obeys God by loving His Son and following His Word, one glorifies the Lord and tastes the sweetest, richest happiness known to man. This and no other substitute is the good life. It is what God has always intended for mankind.

The Good Life Does Not Destroy Self-Love

In unfurling his vision of the good life, Edwards had to overcome a second objection. He had to show how the God-centered life corresponded with the natural human instinct to love and preserve oneself, which he defined as follows: "Self-love, I think, is generally defined: a man's love of his own happiness" (*Works* 8, 575). Did living for God, in other words, mean that one had to sacrifice concern for oneself and adopt a pattern of living that impeded happiness for the sake of obeying God?

Edwards had a ready answer to this question. He refused, at the start, to separate love for God and love for oneself. One best loved oneself by loving God. Loving oneself without God meant that one strayed from the source of all wisdom and truth, and thus consigned oneself to destruction. On the contrary, loving oneself through loving God meant that one experienced the joys of the virtuous life. Instead of living selfishly, mankind could live for God and experience His boundless goodness. In doing so, they would actually care for themselves far better than if they ignored the Lord and went their own way.

Edwards, we see, also refused to separate happiness from obedience. He argued that exercising virtue in service to God actually enabled a person to love themselves best. "True virtue," he argued in *Dissertation Concerning the Nature of True Virtue*, "most essentially consists in benevolence to Being in general. Or perhaps to speak more accurately, it is that consent, propensity and union of heart to Being in general, that is immediately exercised in a general good will" (*Works* 8, 540). The "Being" of which Edwards spoke was God and the system of creaturely being He had created. Living a life of "benevolence" (or loving goodwill) toward God and His creatures meant that one possessed "true virtue." Virtue and happiness actually went hand in hand. When one acted virtuously to others out of a desire to love God and preserve his soul, he found true happiness. Happiness did not come from gratification of one's selfish instincts, but rather from one's desire to bless others and please the Lord.

In the final analysis, Edwards revealed that virtue and self-preservation did not naturally conflict. God designed man to be good. When a person acts on these instincts and lives a life of "benevolence" to God and, accordingly, to his fellow man, he preserves his soul and, as a result, loves himself more than the person who lives without virtue and who operates out of selfishness. Christianity, the life of Spirit-empowered virtue, does not require that one sacrifice happiness. As a believer in Christ lives the good life of obedience to the Lord, he tastes true and lasting happiness, blesses God and mankind, and ultimately preserves his soul. Edwards's doctrine expresses on a theological level the simple truth taught by Christ centuries before in Matthew 16:25: "Whoever would save his life will lose it, but whoever loses his life for my sake will find it."

A Deeply Ironic Doctrine

The Edwardsean doctrine of happiness is rich with irony. To save one's soul and experience deepest delight one must abandon the instinct to selfishly pursue one's well-being. True self-interest involves turning one's life over to God and accepting His plan for life over against anything the human mind can conceive. One cannot win salvation and happiness for oneself by selfish cunning or slick plans. If one desires to know happiness in this life and the next, one must hand one's life over to the Lord. A Christian is a person who hands the keys over to Jesus. The believer trusts Him to lead and guide, knowing that whatever way He directs will be best.

It may not always appear this way, of course. One may trust Christ and find that the going soon gets rough. This is no indication that Christ has failed and that happiness is lost.

While God often allows His children to feel happy because of favorable circumstances, His fundamental gift to believers is not the promise of a life without challenges, but a state of deep happiness rooted in Himself that transcends all situations, good or ill. This is the kind of happiness that lasts beyond a mood or an emotional high. It is a persevering, bold happiness that is rooted in faith in God and love for God.

Some people who know this Edwardsean kind of happiness, this rich brand of spiritual joy, express it with great emotion. Edwards himself regularly experienced a sort of rapturous communion with God. Others, however, express their joy in quieter form, their deep satisfaction in Him manifesting itself in a quiet, contented way of life. Neither mode is best; both are valid and good. The challenge for most of us is to find the happiness common to both groups of happy believers. Too many Christians fail to taste the profound satisfaction offered them in the gospel. They have a sense of their salvation, but they have little awareness of the greatness of the gospel and its ability to altogether transform their existence. They know that God wants them to be happy, but they have not realized that joy comes not primarily from having one's desires met by God, but by serving God and doing what He desires.

Life in Uncomfortable Tension

Too many of us live in a strenuous push-and-pull relationship with the Lord. We obey Him, to some extent, but we also push for the accomplishment of our plans, the fulfillment of our desires, not realizing that He has a better plan and better desires for us. The happiest Christians are not those who manage to accomplish all of their personal goals. Rather, the happiest Christians are those who embrace what God wants for their lives. Thus the irony of faith reveals itself once again. One does not become happy by liberating oneself from duty; one becomes happy by obeying and following the plans of the Lord, who in turn provides the happiness one naturally desires. In duty, in serving the Lord, we find true happiness.

In his sermon "Charity Contrary to a Selfish Spirit," Edwards highlighted this theme as he exhorted his Northampton congregation to live charitably, or lovingly, with their fellow men. He taught them that their performance of charity would not diminish their own happiness, but would increase it to a depth that they had never thought possible. Fundamentally, said the pastor:

A CHRISTIAN SPIRIT SEEKS to please and glorify God. The things which are well pleasing to God and Christ, and tend to the glory of Christ, are called the things of Jesus Christ in opposition to our own things. Philippians 2:21, "For all seek their own, not the things which are Jesus Christ's." Christianity requires that we should make God and Christ our main end. Christians, so far as they live like Christians, live so that for them to live is Christ [Philippians 1:21]. Christians are required to live so as to please God. Romans 12:2, "That ye may prove what is that good, and acceptable, and perfect will of God." We should be such servants of Christ as do in all things seek to please our Master. Ephesians 6:6, "Not with eye-service as men-pleasers: but as the servants of Christ, doing the will of God from the heart." So we are required to seek the glory of God. 1 Corinthians 10:31, "Whether therefore ye eat, or drink, or whatsoever ye do, do all to the glory of God." And this is the Christian spirit. (*Works* 8, 259)

Having defined "the Christian spirit" as that which "seeks to please and glorify God," Edwards discussed how divine love far exceeds natural "self-love":

BUT DIVINE LOVE or that Christian charity which is spoken of in the text is something above self-love, as it is supernatural or above and beyond all that is natural. It is no branch which springs out of that root of self-love as natural affection and civil friendship, and the love which wicked men may have one to another. It is something of a higher and more noble kind. Self-love is the sum of natural principles, as divine love is of supernatural principles. This divine love is no plant which grows naturally in such a soil as the heart of man. But it is a plant transplanted into the soul out of heaven; it is something divine, something from the holy and blessed Spirit of God, and so has its foundation in God, and not in self. (*Works* 8, 263-4)

Edwards provides a memorable image to describe the source of charity. The love in a Christian's heart "is a plant transplanted into the soul out of heaven." This plant, a gift from "the holy and blessed Spirit of God," causes the believer to live for God with God squarely in one's line of sight. As one matures, one's love for God and His creation spills over into the lives of others, just as a maturing plant or tree stretches across an ever-widening distance and shelters it. The believer who seeks to live for God ultimately cannot avoid blessing others.

Edwards next sketched how believers could embody this spirit:

> A CHRISTIAN SPIRIT DISPOSES them in many cases to forego and part with their own things for the sake of the things of others. It disposes them to part with their own private temporal interest, and totally and finally to renounce it, for the sake of the honor of God and the advancement of the kingdom of Christ. Such was the spirit of the Apostle. Acts 21:13, "I am ready not only to be bound, but also to die for the name of the Lord Jesus." And they have a spirit to forego and part with their own private interest for the good of their neighbors in many instances; ready to help bear others' burdens, to part with a less good of their own for the sake of a greater of their neighbors'; and as the case may be, to lay down their lives for the brethren [1 John 3:16]. (*Works* 8, 259)

The pastor closed with a stirring summation of the nature and power of Christian charity:

AND THEREFORE DIVINE and Christian love, above all love in the world, is contrary to a selfish spirit. Though other-love, a moral love, may in some respects be contrary to selfishness, as it may move men to a moral liberality and generosity, yet in other respects it agrees with a selfish spirit; because if we follow it up to its original, it arises from the same root, viz. a principle of self-love. But divine love has its spring elsewhere; its root is in Christ Jesus, and so is heavenly. It is not anything of this world, and it tends thither whence it comes. As it does not spring out of self, so neither does it tend to self. It delights in the honor and glory of God for his own sake, and not merely for their sakes. And it seeks and delights in the good of men for their sakes, and for God's sake. How Christian love is in a pecu-liar manner above and contrary to a selfish spirit appears by this, viz. it goes out even to enemies. There is that in the nature and tendency of it to go out to the unthankful and evil, and to those that injure and hate us, which is directly contrary to the tendency of a selfish principle, and quite above nature. (*Works* 8, 264)

In these sections, Edwards captured the special nature of Christian happiness. Rooted in "divine love," Christians act out of an "other-love" that simultaneously blesses their fellow man and cares for their own soul. In doing so, they find true and lasting happiness. This brand of existence counters sharply the thinking of sinful natural man, which is driven by a selfish and deeply proud mind-set. The Christian life, the good life, is driven by a selfless and humble mindset. Though it might seem natural to devote all kinds of attention to one's own needs, the Christian goes the opposite way and humbly seeks to serve even his enemies. Here is love that turns the thinking of the natural mind on its head. Love of this kind is both deeply ironic and unquestionably divine.

The Happiest Person Who Ever Lived

Edwards's doctrine of happiness and the good life helps us to see how Jesus Christ, despite all the injustices thrust upon Him, was the happiest person who ever lived. Christ devoted every second of His life to serving God and blessing His people. Though He often faced great trials, Jesus knew a satisfaction that no human hand could diminish. Even in His agonizing crucifixion, Jesus rested firmly in the will of God, and endured the agonies of Calvary "for the joy set before Him" (Hebrews 12:2). Though the cross itself produced no happiness in Jesus, submission to God's will did. Christ's example brings home how important it is to understand that happiness is not simply an emotional state. It is both emotion and commitment, both outward exultation and inner satisfaction. As we follow Jesus and obey the Father, serving our fellow man with love in our hearts, we make ourselves happy in the most profound sense, just like Jesus Himself.

We should emphasize that we are not constructing a merely intellectual argument here. There is delight of the most intense and lasting kind in vibrant Christian faith. At one point in his sermon corpus, Edwards went so far as to say that the goodness of Christianity is such that even if Christianity is not true, it still provides the best way to live. It is such a pleasant way to live that it would be the best lifestyle even if the Bible were not true. "Seeing it is so," the pastor concluded in his sermon entitled "The Pleasantness of Religion," "that 'tis worth the while to be religious if it were only for the delight and pleasantness of it, then hence we may learn that sinners are left without any manner of objection against religion" (Kimnach, 23). Edwards believed firmly that Christianity offered humanity the deepest pleasure possible. Even the most apparently happy worldly life could not compare to biblical faith:

> [H]OW EXCEEDING GREAT is the reward of the godly. What a reward have they in the world to come; what joys [in another life]. But yet this is not all; no, they have a reward in this life. In the very keeping of God's commands, there is great reward (Ps. 19:11). The reward they have in hand, besides that which is promised, is well worth all the pains

> they take, all the troubles they endure. God has not only
> promised them a great reward, and exceeding great beyond
> conception; but he has given them a foretaste in this world.
> And this taste is better than all the pleasure and riches of
> the wicked. (Kimnach, 24)

The Christian faith was true, according to Edwards. He made
this very clear in countless sermons and writings. It yielded
both a joyful earthly life and an endlessly happy existence in
heaven. In comparison to the richest sinner, even the poorest
Christian possessed wealth beyond belief. While the "wicked"
courted temporal pleasure, the Christian experienced in the
good life a "foretaste" of heaven that nothing could ruin or
spoil.

The Northampton pastor's preaching illuminated the
divine nature of earthly Christian life. All who would follow
Christ would find that it not only satisfied the soul on earth,
but placed them on the trajectory of heaven. Though this
world dealt "pains" and "troubles" to the people of God,
Edwards knew that these things would soon pass, and the
church would reach its destination, tasting sumptuous
delights not even the richest pleasure-seeker could imagine.

The Happiness of the Good Life

All of the preceding material shapes and perhaps alters
our understanding of Jonathan Edwards. The man who wears
the slightest of smiles in his portrait may not be the vindictive,

pleasure-squashing parson some imagine him to be. Edwards's conception of the good life suggests that Edwards was much happier than we might initially think. Certainly, life as he pictured it in its ideal form reflected an existence of the most satisfied kind. This life, as we have seen, was no exercise in sinful hedonism, but was instead a lifelong walk of faith on the biblical path. This life glorified God and made men happy. It did not conflict with self-interest, it included continual service to God and man, and it required humility and sacrifice. The good life included noteworthy irony that turned conventional human wisdom on its head. It was demanding, challenging, and deeply involved, yet it offered humanity the opportunity to taste the very goodness and love and peace of God.

Such was life as God created it to be.

 *Living the Good Life*

We Are Made to Be Happy

*I*t is imperative that we realize that God has not designed us for a somber, miserable subsistence of a life. He has made us to be unshakably happy. Our first order of business in processing Edwards's illumination of this biblical teaching is to enter the thought stream of our minds, so to speak, and to banish any thinking that undermines the idea that God wants us to be happy in Him. He does not want to squelch our pleasure, and He does not parse out a crumb of blessing at a time for us to sample. God intends to pour a flood of happiness into our lives, and He will do so if we only recognize that this is so (Psalm 128; Jeremiah 32:36–41).

This means on a practical level that we must reorient our thoughts, our words, and our actions. We must not doubt our Lord and His good plan for our lives. We should not speak against the Lord and complain to other people about our circumstances. Romans 8:31–39 teaches us that every single thing that occurs in our lives is placed before us to sanctify us and to glorify God. How, then, can we doubt the Lord? We must accept whatever comes from His hand and remember that He has our happiness in mind, not our misery. This reorientation of thinking and acting will help us to switch from a glum, self-defeated way of life into a courageous, defiantly joyful existence that smacks of another world.

Obedience Is Joy

*E*dwards shows us that the happiest people on earth are not those who do whatever they naturally, sinfully want to do, but those who do what God desires. God, being all-wise and all-good, has designed the ideal way of life. This way of life involves obedience, or submission, to the divine will (Ecclesiastes 12:13). Obedience, then, is joy; following God is happiness (see 1 John 3 for a similar theme). Knowing and applying this truth to our lives will free us from thinking that, though saved, we're missing out on the really good stuff of life that the unredeemed around us get to enjoy every day. If we understand that we're heaven bound, and that all our obedience brings both blessing on earth and an eternal reward in the afterlife, we'll avoid much of the doleful thinking of misled Christians. The good stuff, and the good life, is not to be had in the world of sin, but in the world of faith.

Obedience doesn't always *seem* happy. Sometimes, it's very difficult. But the fact that sin is easy and obedience can be difficult does not mean that sin is right and obedience is wrong. We must guard ourselves against an emotionally driven Christianity that operates out of the satisfaction of whatever momentary desire presents itself. The most robust faith will both engage one's emotions, ensuring that we live a genuinely happy life, and motivate us to obey the Word of God, allowing us to avoid the constant ups and downs of a weak-willed Christianity. God, we must remember, desires to pour happiness into our lives. As the accounts of numerous biblical figures show us, when we follow our Savior and live for His glory, shunning worldly temptations that snap at our feet to trap and destroy us, we set ourselves up to receive in this life and the next the blessings of God (see, for example, Genesis 39–47 and Daniel 1–7). Obedience, then, is not a death to vitality, but a means to happiness.

Be Happy in Serving Others

*A*s we orient our lives around obedience to God's Word, we will find that we cannot help but care for God's handiwork in creation. We'll have an increased desire to steward the earth well, but we'll primarily desire to bless the apex of God's creative work, the human race. As those who have been made deeply happy by God, we'll want others to know that same happiness, and to turn away from the sinful patterns of living that promise so much but deliver so little. We'll seek to care for all people by meeting their earthly needs as best we can with wisdom and discernment, and we'll try to tell them about the source of all happiness, God, as He has revealed Himself in His Word (see Luke 10:25–37, for example, and Galatians 6:10). The ways in which Christians share the good life and the good news will vary according to place and situation, but all Christians who desire to be truly happy will channel their love for God into evangelistic service to their fellow man. This is not some kind of programmatic requirement that believers fulfill, but is a natural overflow of the love for God and His creation that the Spirit of God creates in a believer's heart. Christians should seek opportunities for evangelism and action in their local church, using it as a base from which to work.

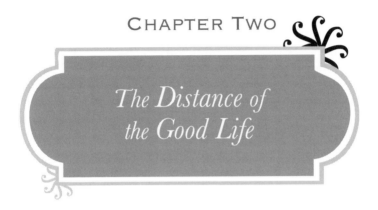

CHAPTER TWO

*The Distance of
the Good Life*

The scenario is all too familiar. We have all seen it play out. A person with great potential rises to the surface, promising great things by their gifting and background: a flash of genius, a stunning performance, a thrilling creation. Whether working in the field of art, music, literature, sports, politics, or many others, this person creates a buzz and draws a crowd. Suddenly, everyone is talking about "the next big thing." This pattern characterizes a world that often cares more for that which dazzles—personality, wit, looks—than substantive things like character.

How disappointing it is when the rising star falls, as so many do. No matter how much attention they initially receive, few people in this world seem able to live up to the standards set before them. The promising actor falters in a role or two and ends up on a reality TV show. The electrifying politician exhibits questionable morality and disappears from view. The can't-miss quarterback falls into a slump and his endorsers slink away. In these and similar instances, we glimpse one of the recurring themes of this fallen, broken world: a person failing to live up to the lofty goal for which they were destined and equipped.

As Jonathan Edwards knew, this theme is as old as the world itself. In his God-centered view of creation, the Lord had created the race of mankind for the purpose of displaying and reflecting His glory. In living out this divine call, mankind faced the prospect of unending happiness and undying satisfaction. God, Edwards taught, had made mankind to be happy, and, most specifically, to be happy in Him. By obeying and serving the Lord and His creation, mankind would know happiness of a heavenly kind. Human life, as we saw in the first chapter, was thus invested with potential of the richest kind, the potential to live in perfect harmony with God, experiencing His goodness and grace for ever and ever.

Yet, the failure of Adam and Eve to avoid the serpent's temptation brought it all to ruin (Genesis 3). When they committed the first human sin, all their potential was scattered to the wind. Mankind, created to abide with God, now roamed the hard ground of earth alone. The fate of humanity, meant to rise into the heavens, plunged into the abyss. God would no longer walk on the earth; now a roaring, blood-hungry devil would scour it for those whom he might destroy. If ever potential crashed and burned, if ever gifting failed to deliver, it was here.

So it was that the good life slipped out of humanity's natural reach. In his writing and preaching, Jonathan Edwards explored this tragedy. He looked into the fall's beginnings and its implications and he offered an explanation for the original sin of Adam and Eve, showing how they, not God, were to blame for it. In doing so, Edwards showed how, in losing fellowship with God, mankind had lost contact with true happiness, the good life intended for God's creation. He revealed that God did not oppose pleasure and joy, but rather disordered, misdirected "happiness." Mankind, Edwards argued, possessed a vast capacity for pleasure, a capacity given it by the Lord. In the wake of the fall, however, only the Holy Spirit's work in the human heart could direct it to the rightful fulfillment of this capacity.

In the mystery and miracle of divine grace, the fallen race of man could rise once more. Unlike the disgraced and disappointing leaders and celebrities so familiar to our age, human beings could reclaim their purpose, their place in the world, and the happiness God intended them to have. In this chapter, we explore Edwards's conception of the fall, its effects on the human race, and the state of sin-clouded affections. We will examine Edwards's treatment of these subjects in his classic works *Original Sin* and *Religious Affections.* In the process, we will see how humanity has lost the good life, and what must happen before we can experience it again and find true happiness in this broken place.

Edwards's Doctrine of Sin

To comprehend the sad condition of the human race and its vast natural distance from the life of happiness God intended for it, it is first necessary to review Edwards's basic understanding of sin. In studying it, we find the reason for the unhappiness of this world. The pastor worked through his doctrine of sin most substantively in the book *Original Sin*, where he offered his basic definition of the title subject: "By original sin, as the phrase has been most commonly used by divines, is meant the *innate sinful depravity of the heart*" (*Works* 3, 107). For Edwards, original sin was most fundamentally a disposition of the heart that manifested itself in wicked acts. As he countered the arguments of some who denied the existence of original sin, he pointed out that Scripture overwhelmingly substantiated the idea. One simply could not profess to follow the Bible and deny the innate sinfulness and guilt of all people, said Edwards:

> THAT EVERY ONE OF MANKIND, at least of them that are capable of acting as moral agents, are guilty of sin (not now taking it for granted that they come guilty into the world) is a thing most clearly and abundantly evident from the holy Scriptures. (1 Kings 8:46), "If any man sin against thee, for there is no man that sinneth not." (Ecclesiastes 7:20), "There is not a just man upon earth that doeth good, and sinneth not." (Job 9:2–3), "I know it is so of a truth" (i.e. as

Bildad had just before said, that God would not cast away a perfect man, etc.), "but how should man be just with God? If he will contend with him, he cannot answer him one of a thousand." To the like purpose (Psalms 143:2), "Enter not into judgment with thy servant; for in thy sight shall no man living be justified." So the words of the Apostle (in which he has apparent reference to those words of the Psalmist, Romans 3:19–20), "That every mouth may be stopped, and all the world become guilty before God. Therefore by the deeds of the law there shall no flesh be justified in his sight: for by the law is the knowledge of sin." . . . All are represented, not only as being sinful, but as having great and manifold iniquity (Job 9:2, Job 9:3; James 3:1, James 3:2). (*Works* 3, 114–15)

To summarize the point and make it even clearer, Edwards reiterated that sin proceeded from *every* human heart:

IN GOD'S SIGHT NO MAN LIVING can be justified; but all are sinners, and exposed to condemnation. This is true of persons of all constitutions, capacities, conditions, manners, opinions and educations; in all countries, climates, nations and ages; and through all the mighty changes and revolutions, which have come to pass in the habitable world. (*Works* 3, 124)

With his methodical mind, Edwards first established that sin existed and that it came directly from the hearts of people. Over against some who contended that sin was more an external matter than an internal one, the Northampton theologian asserted that the Bible abounded with condemnation of all people. His treatment makes clear that the Bible deals constantly with sin. From one angle or another, the authors of Scripture return over and over to the concept. Prophets denounce kings for adultery, kings denounce prophets for laxity, priests make sacrifices for the nation, the nation suffers from wicked priests. In these and a thousand other ways, the Bible addresses sin. It is not too much to say, presumably with Edwards, that it is in one sense a book about sin.

No person, furthermore, can escape the presence of sin. Every person nurses it in their heart, regardless of their "constitutions, capacities, conditions, manners, opinions and educations." Those of "all countries, climates, nations and ages" carry sin in their core. With a flurry of terms, Edwards reinforced his point, leaving none outside of the sphere of sin, implicating all as guilty. His words, unpopular in his day, are no more popular in ours, however staunchly supported they were and are by even a brief glance at world affairs and personal circumstances.

The God-Defying Nature of Sin

Having established the reality of sin and its widespread nature, Edwards ramped up his discussion, showing that sin is so heinous because it offends God and refuses Him the respect and obedience He deserves:

> THE HEINOUSNESS OF THIS must rise in some proportion to the obligation we are under to regard the Divine Being; and that must be in some proportion to his worthiness of regard; which doubtless is infinitely beyond the worthiness of any of our fellow creatures. But the merit of our respect or obedience to God is not infinite. The merit of respect to any being don't increase, but is rather diminished in pro-portion to the obligations we are under in strict justice to pay him that respect. There is no great merit in paying a debt we owe, and by the highest possible obligations in strict justice are obliged to pay; but there is great demerit in refusing to pay it. (*Works* 3, 130)

The argument corrects the mistaken claim that human good-ness can counterbalance human sin and overcome it in the eyes of God. God, Edwards pointed out, deserves not finite respect, but "infinite." The best we humans can offer, how-ever, is "respect or obedience to God [that] is not infinite." This difficulty is compounded by the fact that we not only fall short of paying our debt of righteousness to God, but also often "refus[e] to pay" that which in "highest possible obliga-tions in strict justice" we "are obliged to pay." We do God no favor in seeking to honor Him; He deserves our honor. But without the righteousness of Christ, even our best efforts to honor Him fall utterly short of the mark.

Edwards advanced the discussion further, insisting that we are not merely obligated to honor God, but to go beyond mere performance of duty and love Him with our hearts. This duty is not arbitrarily imposed; that is, it does not flow out of some artificial, purposeless law. We are called to love God because of who God is in Himself. Edwards writes:

HOW FAR THE GENERALITY of mankind are from their duty with respect to love to God, will further appear, if we consider, that we are obliged not only to love him with a love of gratitude for benefits received; but true love to God primarily consists in a supreme regard to him for what he is in himself. . . . If God be infinitely excellent in himself, then he is infinitely lovely on that account; or in other words, infinitely worthy to be loved. And doubtless, if he be worthy to be loved for this, then he ought to be loved for this. And 'tis manifest, there can be no true love to him, if he be not loved for what he is in himself. For if we love him not for his own sake, but for something else, then our love is not terminated on him, but on something else, as its ultimate object. . . . If we love not God because he is what he is, but only because he is profitable to us, in truth we love him not at all. If we seem to love him, our love is not to him, but to something else. (*Works* 3, 144)

Here Edwards lays bare the depravity of human sin. Humanity transgressed against God by not doing what He desires—true; by not respecting as He deserves—yes; but most damningly, by not obeying Him out of a heart justifiably filled with love and adoration for who He is. Here is wickedness at its core and rebellion at its worst. Though mankind had every reason to trust and love God, he chose not to in the wake of Adam's fall. Choosing to love lesser things and live a lesser life, he resigned himself to sadness and death.

The Inferior and Superior Principles

But why did man choose such a path, and hurtle himself toward hell in the process? Why did Adam and Eve choose to sin against God despite having every reason to follow Him and shun the serpent? To this question Edwards's creative mind produced a compelling answer that forms the crux of this chapter and reveals the ultimate source of earthly unhappiness. In the following quotation, the theologian suggests that God created Adam with two different "principles," as he calls them. The first was the "inferior"—spiritually neutral principles that included man's "natural appetites and passions." The second was the "superior"—those that "were spiritual, holy and divine." Edwards discussed each kind in *Original Sin*:

> The case with man was plainly this: when God made man
> at first, he implanted in him two kinds of principles. There
> was an *inferior* kind, which may be called *natural*, being the

> principles of mere human nature; such as self-love, with
> those natural appetites and passions, which belong to the
> nature of man, in which his love to his own liberty, honor
> and pleasure, were exercised: these when alone, and left to
> themselves, are what the Scriptures sometimes call flesh.
> Besides these, there were superior principles, that were
> spiritual, holy and divine, summarily comprehended in
> divine love; wherein consisted the spiritual image of God,
> and man's righteousness and true holiness; which are
> called in Scripture the divine nature. (*Works* 3, 381)

God had created man with "mere human nature," which con-
sisted of the natural principles, the natural instincts, and dis-
positions of man—his drive to eat, reproduce, work, and so
on all fell in this category. Though these instincts certainly
could involve spiritual evil or good, they were at base neutral,
neither infused with sin nor grace. Man in his natural state,
in his "flesh," was thus subject neither to condemnation or
blessed immortality. The supernatural principles residing in
him—characteristics of a "spiritual, holy, and divine" orienta-
tion—came from God Himself.

The Consequences of the Fall

The fall occurred when the inferior principles, the flesh,
overtook the superior or supernatural principles, the spirit, as
Edwards spelled out:

THESE SUPERIOR PRINCIPLES were given to possess the
throne, and maintain an absolute dominion in the heart:
the other, to be wholly subordinate and subservient. And
while things continued thus, all things were in excellent
order, peace and beautiful harmony, and in their proper
and perfect state. These divine principles thus reigning,
were the dignity, life, happiness, and glory of man's nature.
When man sinned, and broke God's Covenant, and fell
under his curse, these superior principles left his heart: for
indeed God then left him; that communion with God, on
which these principles depended, entirely ceased; the Holy
Spirit, that divine inhabitant, forsook the house. Because it
would have been utterly improper in itself, and inconsis-
tent with the covenant and constitution God had established, that God should still maintain communion with
man, and continue, by his friendly, gracious vital influences,
to dwell with him and in him, after he was become a rebel,
and had incurred God's wrath and curse. Therefore immediately the superior divine principles wholly ceased; so
light ceases in a room, when the candle is withdrawn: and
thus man was left in a state of darkness, woeful corruption
and ruin; nothing but flesh, without spirit.

Edwards explained the effects of this disastrous shift:

THE INFERIOR PRINCIPLES of self-love and natural appetite, which were given only to serve, being alone, and left to themselves, of course became reigning principles; having no superior principles to regulate or control them, they became absolute masters of the heart. The immediate consequence of which was a fatal catastrophe, a turning of all things upside down, and the succession of a state of the most odious and dreadful confusion. Man did immediately set up himself, and the objects of his private affections and appetites, as supreme; and so they took the place of God. (*Works* 3, 382)

Edwards's language captures the chilling instance when, for the first time in creation, the inferior principles, "given" to man "only to serve" him (by providing for his natural, neutral appetites) overthrew the superior principles and "became absolute masters of the heart." In that moment, "man did immediately set up himself . . . as supreme" and sought "the place of God." Thousands of years after the event, one's blood still grows cold while meditating on it. Seeking to become all-wise, humanity in fact became stupid; chasing immortal life, mankind seized hold of eternal death.

Where Was God in the Fall?

Anticipating questions that would naturally flow from this argument, the pastor next considered God's role in those events. If God was sovereign, as Edwards so strenuously insisted he was, why did man fall? For this Edwards had a ready answer. It was not God's direct action but His permission that was operative:

> THE FIRST EXISTENCE of an evil disposition of heart, amounting to a full consent to Adam's sin, no more infers God's being the author of that evil disposition in the child, than in the father. The first arising or existing of that evil disposition in the heart of Adam, was by God's *permission*; who could have prevented it, if he had pleased, by giving such influences of his spirit, as would have been absolutely effectual to hinder it; which, it is plain in fact, he did withhold: and whatever mystery may be supposed in the affair, yet no Christian will presume to say, it was not in perfect consistence with God's holiness and righteousness, notwithstanding Adam had been guilty of no offense before. So root and branches being one, according to God's wise constitution, the case in fact is, that by virtue of this oneness answerable changes of effects through all the branches coexist with the changes in the root: consequently an evil disposition exists in the hearts of Adam's posterity, equivalent to that which was exerted in his own heart, when he eat the forbidden fruit. Which God has no hand in, any otherwise, than in not exerting such an influence, as might be effectual to prevent it. (*Works* 3, 394)

The "permission" of God, not the active decree of His will, enabled the fall of mankind. The theologian acknowledged that the Lord "could have prevented it, if he had pleased," but did not. "God ha[d] no hand" in this matter, according to Edwards, other than to "not exert an influence" that would have prevented it. His conclusion, therefore, was that a) man caused the fall, b) God could have prevented it but did not, and c) that the workings of this difficult situation were a mystery best left to the mind of God and not the speculation of man. Edwards held the fall of man and the sovereignty of God in tension, emphasizing each in turn as directed by the Scripture, but allowing for mystery due to the finitude of human understanding.

Inheriting the Fall

The tragic effects of the fall extended not only to Adam and Eve but to all their "posterity," every person who would ever live. On the question of why God allowed the fall, the council of the divine mind hid itself; on the matter of humanity's wickedness, the depravity of the human race showed itself plainly. Because they ate the forbidden fruit, "consequently an evil disposition exists in the hearts" of all mankind. "[T]he depravity of nature," Edwards said elsewhere, "remaining an *established principle* in the heart of a child of Adam, and as exhibited in after-operations, is a consequence and punishment of the first apostasy thus participated, and brings new guilt" (*Works* 3, 391). Every person stands guilty before

God as a result of the representative role Adam occupied before the Lord. Yet he did not merely represent humanity in the presence of God; when he sinned, he actually passed on his "apostasy" and "guilt" to all people in an organic, holistic way. All people inherited a sin nature at birth, and could do nothing to overturn the curse and its effects.

Why Satisfaction Escapes Us

All of this leaves us with an answer to the enigma of man's unhappiness and inability to find satisfaction. When our first parents sinned by eating the forbidden fruit, they ensured that for all of time, the inferior principles, not the superior principles, would govern the human heart. The flesh, in short, would forever rule the spirit. Man did not lose his conscience in this instance. But he did lose his ability to obey his conscience consistently. In this awful condition, he could glimpse that a higher, better, way of life existed than that which he chose, but he could never lay hold of it, and he often did not want to, preferring the filth of his natural, sin-driven lifestyle. He could see, fleetingly, that true happiness existed, but could not capture it. Instead of loving what was good and true and beautiful, he ran wherever his sinful, selfish appetites drove him. Because of the first sin, and the transmission of a sinful nature to all people, our natural principles rule us and subject us to unhappiness, despair, death, and ultimately, eternal death.

The Difference between
"True" and "False" Affections

What, then, does all of the preceding show? We were not created for this. God did not intend our lives to take this shape, to play this tragic tune. He gave us natural desires and instincts that He intended to be vessels of pleasure and satisfaction for us. He gave us what Edwards called "affections," natural passions that He desired we direct toward Him in joyful worship. With the fall, we did not lose our desires and affections. Instead, the sin of Adam and Eve disordered our affections, confused them, and caused us to love sin and hate God. In essence, where once the spiritual, or superior, principles ruled the affections, now the inferior, fleshly, principles directed them. In a section in his treatise *Religious Affections*, the pastor discussed this situation. He showed that there are two types of affections, "false" and "true":

THERE ARE FALSE AFFECTIONS, and there are true. A man's having much affection, don't prove that he has any true religion: but if he has no affection, it proves that he has no true religion. The right way, is not to reject all affections, nor to approve all; but to distinguish between affections, approving some, and rejecting others; separating between the wheat and the chaff, the gold and the dross, the precious and the vile.

Edwards believed some in his day were trying to remove all sense of emotion and pleasure from religion—a shift he denounced:

> THIS MANNER OF SLIGHTING all religious affections, is the way exceedingly to harden the hearts of men, and to encourage 'em in their stupidity and senselessness, and to keep 'em in a state of spiritual death as long as they live, and bring 'em at last to death eternal. The prevailing prejudice against religious affections at this day, in the land, is apparently of awful effect, to harden the hearts of sinners, and damp the graces of many of the saints, and stunt the life and power of religion, and preclude the effect of ordinances, and hold us down in a state of dullness and apathy, and undoubtedly causes many persons greatly to offend God, in entertaining mean and low thoughts of the extraordinary work he has lately wrought in this land. (*Works* 2, 121)

He then restated the effect of such a deplorable approach to the affections: "for persons to despise and cry down all religious affections, is the way to shut all religion out of their own hearts, and to make thorough work in ruining their souls" (*Works* 2, 121). To summarize these quotations, Edwards believed that God had given mankind feelings and emotions. These natural passions were not sinful, wrong, or destined to be destroyed by conversion. God, in Edwards's thinking, did not wish to remove feeling—and feeling of the deepest, strongest sort—from the redeemed life. Those who argued that line, contended the pastor, would "harden the hearts of sinners, and damp the graces of many of the saints, and stunt the life and power of religion." As one can see, Edwards held nothing back in his denunciation of a passionless Christianity. His life shows that he made it a key part of his pastoral and theological work to exalt the goodness of feeling and true passion for God. He had his qualifiers and exceptions, to be sure, but Jonathan Edwards believed ardently that God had given the human race feelings and passion to experience the full range of joy and delight in Him. In Edwards's day, as in other times, God had done "extraordinary work," which deserved not lightly murmured thanks but an explosion of gratitude and praise.

Unlike what some urged in Edwards's day (and ours), the secret of vibrant and effective Christianity centered in its *sanctification* of our natural appetites and passions, not the *squandering* of the same. It was not emotion and passion that needed correcting, but *sinful* emotion and *transgressive* passion. Godly emotion and Christ-centered passion went up as a sweet savor to the Lord.

All this clarifies the Christian's duty and approach to the non-Christian. The Lord calls us, in a sense, to be emissaries of true passion, ambassadors of lasting delight to unconverted people. We do not approach unbelievers with the mindset that they need to repent of their emotions. Rather, we share with the lost that they need to repent of their *sin*, and that they need to redirect their joy, delight, affection, happiness, and satisfaction toward God and the things of God. The lost, in sum, need to leave "false" affections, passions rooted in sin, and take up "true" affections, passions rooted in God and ever-lasting delight.

A Reconceptualization of Evangelism and Christian Life

Edwards's material clarifies the nature of Christian evangelism and, even more, the Christian life. God does not redeem us to save us from pleasure. He is not seeking to scrub happiness from the earth. God redeems us to *give* us pleasure and to make us happy. He wishes to satisfy us at the core of our being, to bring peace to our mind and happiness to our souls through His Spirit. He wants to give not a trickle of blessing mixed with tons of rules, but a flood of happiness that pours into our hearts and minds and that bursts out of us through our affections and our joyful stewardship of our appetites. God, in sum, has made us to be happy above all. He will do so if we allow Him the opportunity.

This carries tremendous implications for our evangelism. Edwards teaches us that we do not contact the lost to tell them *only* that they are sinning and live in danger of the mighty wrath of God, though this is certainly an essential part of Christian witness. Instead, we must give attention in our evangelism to informing unsaved people that they need not lose many of their passions and appetites (though some must go), but that such passions need to be redirected according to the righteous and beneficial plan of Scripture.

At this point in their lives, the lost act according to the inferior principles. They are ruled by them. They have lost the superior principles and, accordingly, possess misdirected affections and appetites. They must now embrace the Holy Spirit and His regenerating work and watch as the spiritual principles, the superior graces given by God, take root in their hearts. Much more will be said on this in the following chapters; here, we simply state the reality and the need every heart has for this transformation. Without the Spirit's restoration of the reign of the superior principles, we cannot know true happiness, and we cannot please God, but only bring great suffering to ourselves and great dishonor to the Lord.

Attaining the Good Life

In conclusion, we see what great potential every person has. We are not referring here to athletic or intellectual ability, nor artistic or political capacity. We signify the deepest potential, the spiritual, which pervades every aspect of a person's being. Human beings have the ability, if they follow the Word of God according to the Spirit of God, to transcend this world, to triumph over their sin, and to enter the presence of God. We alone among all the creation may live forever. We alone may taste the very goodness and happiness of God. We were, after all, created to do so. Yet at present, our sin has confused us, impeded our happiness, disordered our experience. We live in unhappiness, gratifying our appetites and pleasing our passions in ungodly ways. None of us can escape this fate; all of us receive it from our parents and pass it on to our children.

But we may yet fulfill our potential, our purpose, for life. We may find the satisfaction we have always sought. We can conquer disappointment, doubt, and the last enemy, death. If we will follow the Lord and His Word, our highest virtue and greatest happiness will come together in the Spirit-filled life God intends us to experience.

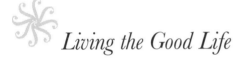

Living the Good Life

Realize the Nature and Power of Sin

*E*dwards's understanding of the fall, consonant with traditional understandings but more fully explored than some, shows us the depth of our depravity. Sin, fundamentally, is not loving God. In all of our offenses, we in some way fail to love and treasure God. We break God's rules, yes; we fail to live up to His standards. But why do we do so? Because we do not love God enough. We hate Him by nature (see Psalm 51:5; Jeremiah 17:9; Romans 3).

This has strong implications for our everyday lives. Why do we live selfishly with our spouse? Because we don't love God and His gift of a spouse enough. Why do we turn in a substandard performance day after day at work or school? Because we don't love God and His blessing of provision or education enough. Why do we fight with our friends, disobey our parents, squander our talents? Because we don't love God and His tangible expressions of kindness. Sure, there are psychological and other factors that play into our patterns of sin—some of them significant—but we need to know that our fundamental problem is not psychological or external, but spiritual (see Psalm 14:1). If we loved God rightly, we would follow Him thoroughly, and we would see all that He places in our path as good (Romans 8:31–39). Because we do not love God rightly, we rebel against Him and His design, choosing selfishly, living narcissistically, trudging blindly through our days. Sin is powerful, and if we allow it, it will cause us to lose our love for God and to chase after fleeting, empty things. We must know this, and we must pursue friendships, accountability, and instruction that will, above all else, direct us Godward and cause us to pulse with love for our Savior, who gives every good gift and loves to bless His children (James 1:17).

Know the Goodness of Your Passions and Appetites

*T*hroughout history, Christians have sometimes reacted against the excesses of their day by retreating into moralism and prudery. That is, faced with a decadent culture, they have turned a cold shoulder to the idea of pleasure and bodily fulfillment. Though such a posture is understandable in certain circumstances, it may also be regrettable. As Edwards shows us plainly, the fall did not destroy the passions and appetites God created, but rather misdirected them.

When the Spirit regenerates us, He enables us to use our natural passions and appetites according to the superior, not the inferior, principles. As Christians, we must recognize this and avoid misrepresenting God and the good life. The ideal Christian life is not a prim, stifling affair in which we moralistically perform righteousness for the Lord as joylessly as possible. The ideal Christian life, the good life God intends for us, is a joyful, pleasurable, happy affair in which we shun sin and seek holiness because we treasure God and desire to taste His goodness in all facets of our lives. We pursue holiness with abandon, but we do so in full view of the expressed mercy of the cross. We live sacrificially and in moderation, but also treasure our bodies and the good gifts available to us on this earth. Swept up in happiness, we exude not a self-righteous, judgmental spirit but a deep joy rooted in conviction and love for God and man. This kind of life is available to all of us, but many of us practice a deficient Christianity ruled less by grace and more by rules, less by happiness and more by performance. As pastor Tim Keller has made clear in his writings and teachings (see *The Reason for God*), we are not accepted because we obey; rather, we obey because we are accepted. With this kind of mindset firmly in place, let us outlive the world, treasuring good gifts, pursuing superior pleasures, rightly gratifying the appetites God has given us (see Hebrews 13:9–14).

Call the Lost to Happiness

*A*s we have seen, Edwards's understanding of man's natural appetites and passions transforms our evangelism. We
do not approach people to call them out of happiness and
assign them to a ritualistic, grim existence in which they
please God by mere duty. We reach out to lost people to tell
them that they are letting their inferior principles drive their
appetites and passions, and that if they continue to do so, this
pattern will lead them infinitely and unalterably far from the
presence of God. It is not pleasure and happiness that they
need to give up; it is sin, and the sinfully oriented pleasures
that they seek. We call them to repent of these ways, to for-
sake sin, and to trust Jesus Christ, the Savior who waits to
lead them into pleasures evermore (Psalms 16:11).

This reframes the way that we talk to the people around
us in the most practical of ways. To the hedonistic college stu-
dent indulging her love for partying and sex, we share that
God has created her appetites and passions to find proper,
God-glorifying expression in the covenant of marriage. God
does not intend to squelch her happiness, but to channel it in
ways that stand to bless her and honor Him. To the narcissistic loner who lives a lifestyle that serves only themselves, we
call them to the joy of Christian community, the church,
where they will find far greater delight in serving needy believers than they ever will in catering to their own whims. To the
one who runs hard after economic achievement and success,
we share that God desires to channel their energy and ambi-

tion for the advancement of His kingdom. One can build an earthly empire, yes, and know success and some degree of fulfillment, but this pales in comparison to the joy and satisfaction that come from principled stewardship of one's wealth and strategic, sacrificial giving that will spread the gospel and the good life to every corner of the world.

In your evangelism, then, share the gospel message. But do so with an eye to the particular weaknesses and desires of the individual with whom you talk. Show them that God created their passions and appetites for their good and His glory. Tell them that though they are now ruled by inferior urges, and are experiencing all kinds of disorder, confusion, sadness, and guilt as a result, the Savior stands ready to save them and usher them into the fullness of joy.

CHAPTER THREE

The Taste for the Good Life

*W*hat is the deepest difference between the unbelieving
life and the Christian life?

For Jonathan Edwards, the answer came down to the
affections, the emotions of the heart that fundamentally drive
a person's actions. The difference between heaven and hell,
then, is a matter of heart-disposition, or what could be called
"taste."

We are not accustomed to thinking of spiritual things in
such terms. For us, faith and spirituality relate more to cate-
gories of right and wrong than they do to taste. Taste, that
which one relishes or delights in, conjures up images of fancy
gourmet chefs or overly dramatic stylistas. As many of us see

it, faith and taste do not relate. Christians follow God because, primarily, it is the right thing to do, not because we have a taste for it.

Edwards certainly affirmed that we must worship God because He is true and right and good. But in his writings, the pastor offered a deeper and expanded understanding of the heart of our faith. He argued that the soul takes its direction from the affections, our deepest feelings, since that which we relish, or take delight in, forms our spiritual and intellectual target. If we have a taste for sin, then we follow it, chasing it all the way to the grave. Some of us have great hunger for sex, some for wealth, some for fame, some for isolation, some for power, some for achievement, some for rebellion, some for popularity. Whatever our bent, we naturally indulge it with intensity, creating a lifestyle motivated by sin-tainted appetites and passions that lead us far from the blessing of God.

There are some, though, who by the grace of God acquire a finer taste and a higher target. In a world where so many paths to fulfillment prove imaginary, the Lord opens the eyes of some to see that lasting pleasure does, in fact, exist. To people who once sated their hunger with the junk food of this earth, God imparts a voracious appetite for His personal beauty, truth, and goodness.

Edwards described this newfound appetite in a variety of ways—as a "sense," a "taste," and similar metaphors. In each of them, he sought to capture the essence of conversion. The fundamental mark of the Christian, Edwards argued, was this elevated taste for the things of God. Given by the Holy Spirit through the preaching of the gospel, the taste for divine things redirected one's natural passions and appetites to the spiritual riches of the good life. In this chapter, we examine Edwards's understanding of this taste and its role in conversion, revealing it to be the fundamental mark of regeneration. This chapter surveys a number of important sermons, including "A Divine and Supernatural Light," "The Reality of Conversion," and "The Importance and Advantage of a Thorough Knowledge of Divine Truth." Through engagement with these sermons, we will discover what the taste is, describe how it comes to the sinner, and explore the kind of life it creates. In sum, we find that the Edwardsean material offers a powerful explanation of Christian identity and an invigorating exploration of the blessings of the good life.

The Reorientation of Conversion

As noted above, Edwards discussed in a number of places the way conversion produces reorientation of the affections, the natural appetites, and passions. He presented these ideas with clarity and beauty in the sermon "A Divine and Supernatural Light," where he discussed the "light" imparted to the soul at conversion. First, Edwards discussed the way in which a mere conviction of sin and guilt in the sinner's heart did not equate with repentance:

THOSE CONVICTIONS THAT NATURAL MEN may have of their sin and misery is not this spiritual and divine light.

Men in a natural condition may have convictions of the
guilt that lies upon them, and of the anger of God, and
their danger of divine vengeance. Such convictions are
from light or sensibleness of truth: that some sinners have
a greater conviction of their guilt and misery than others,
is because some have more light, or more of an apprehen-
sion of truth, than others. And this light and conviction
may be from the Spirit of God; the Spirit convinces men of
sin: but yet nature is much more concerned in it than in the
communication of that spiritual and divine light, that is
spoken of in the doctrine; 'tis from the Spirit of God only
as assisting natural principles, and not as infusing any new
principles.

Edwards's argument was that the Holy Spirit could convict a
sinner's conscience, but that this conviction did not regenerate the sinful heart until He wrought a fresh work of grace. He
went on to describe this work as follows:

BUT IN THE RENEWING and sanctifying work of the Holy
Ghost, those things are wrought in the soul that are above
nature, and of which there is nothing of the like kind in the
soul by nature; and they are caused to exist in the soul
habitually, and according to such a stated constitution or
law, that lays such a foundation for exercises in a continued
course, as is called a principle of nature. Not only are

remaining principles assisted to do their work more freely
and fully, but those principles are restored that were utterly
destroyed by the fall; and the mind thenceforward habitually exerts those acts that the dominion of sin had made it
as wholly destitute of, as a dead body is of vital acts. (*Works*
17, 410–11)

This section provides an exquisite description of the effects of
conversion on a person's mind and soul. When the Holy Spirit
moves in a heart to cause it to love Jesus Christ and to believe
in His atoning death and life-giving resurrection, "principles"
that are "above nature" take root. In addition, "remaining principles" are freed "to do their work more freely and fully," by
which Edwards meant that conversion enhanced the natural
appetites and enabled them to function properly. Accordingly,
principles "destroyed by the fall" were "restored" such that the
mind "exerts those acts" of a spiritual, not natural or lowly,
nature.

The Root of True Conversion

Edwards did not spell out *all* of the implications of these
new and revived principles, but he did describe in vivid language
the reality of the transformation wrought in conversion. The
Holy Spirit shone a "spiritual light" in the human heart in conversion, which Edwards defined as "a true sense of the divine
excellency of the things revealed in the Word of God, and a
conviction of the truth and reality of them, thence arising."

He elaborated on this definition, noting that in the "spiritual light" there is:

> A TRUE SENSE OF THE DIVINE and superlative excellency
> of the things of religion; a real sense of the excellency of
> God, and Jesus Christ, and of the work of redemption, and
> the ways and works of God revealed in the gospel. There is
> a divine and superlative glory in these things; an excellency
> that is of a vastly higher kind, and more sublime nature,
> than in other things; a glory greatly distinguishing them
> from all that is earthly and temporal. He that is spiritually
> enlightened truly apprehends and sees it, or has a sense of
> it. He don't merely rationally believe that God is glorious,
> but he has a sense of the gloriousness of God in his heart.
> There is not only a rational belief that God is holy, and that
> holiness is a good thing; but there is a sense of the loveli-
> ness of God's holiness. There is not only a speculatively
> judging that God is gracious, but a sense how amiable God
> is upon that account; or a sense of the beauty of this divine
> attribute. (*Works* 17, 413)

The key distinction in this passage is that of "rational belief" and being "spiritually enlightened." The person who has a rational belief in God rightly comprehends the fundamental facts of God as laid out in the Bible and agrees with them. Many people, as Edwards notes, may believe that "God is holy," but there is a chasm between this type of belief and "a sense of the loveliness of God's holiness." Further in the sermon, the pastor expounded on this point:

> THUS THERE IS A DIFFERENCE between having an opinion that God is holy and gracious, and having a sense of the loveliness and beauty of that holiness and grace. There is a difference between having a rational judgment that honey is sweet, and having a sense of its sweetness. A man may have the former, that knows not how honey tastes; but a man can't have the latter, unless he has an idea of the taste of honey in his mind. So there is a difference between believing that a person is beautiful, and having a sense of his beauty. The former may be obtained by hearsay, but the latter only by seeing the countenance. There is a wide difference between mere speculative, rational judging anything to be excellent, and having a sense of its sweetness, and beauty. The former rests only in the head, speculation only is concerned in it; but the heart is concerned in the latter. When the heart is sensible of the beauty and amiableness of a thing, it necessarily feels pleasure in the apprehension. It is implied in a person's being heartily sensible of the loveliness of a thing, that the idea of it is sweet and pleasant to his soul; which is a far different thing from having a rational opinion that it is excellent. (*Works* 17, 414)

The passage makes an impression through its use of metaphor. In a now famous connection, Edwards likened a saving love of God to a "sense" of the "sweetness" of "honey," by which he meant a delightful partaking of the sweetness of honey. In the same way that one tasted the sweetness of honey for oneself, spooning it out and savoring it on the tongue, believers savor and delight in the sweet "excellency of Christ," finding it the best of all pleasures.

This helps clarify the distinction between rational judgment and affectional tasting. Those who taste the goodness of God as revealed in the gospel of His Son take *pleasure* in Him. They enjoy Him. They delight in Him. Edwards spoke of Christ as "beautiful," intending his hearers to connect God's beauty to the experience of romantic love. His words above remind us quite naturally of a marital relationship in which a husband, for example, gazes on his wife's beauty. In fixing his eyes on her, he does not merely acquire the rational idea that his wife is beautiful. He treasures her; he drinks her in; his rational awareness of her beauty intoxicates him. It is this kind of knowledge that Edwards identifies as the "light," the "sense," the "taste" that the Holy Spirit creates for God in the believing heart. As one can tell, this is no ordinary love. Conversion produces a holy passion for the Lord so strong that one of history's most articulate theologians struggled to describe it.

Edwards's Hunger for His
Church's Lasting Satisfaction

Because of his close spiritual communion with the Lord, Edwards experienced this delight firsthand. He yearned for Christians to leave the junk of this world and to taste the sweet excellency of the divine. His concern for such discovery was intense not only because of his devotion to the Lord but on account the state of the Christian church in New England in his day. Colonial New England did not lack for people who held rational belief in the Bible and its truths. Most people attended church and believed what they heard. But few exhibited a real fire for God. To use a recent metaphor, there were many who knew the nature of honey, but few who had tasted its sweetness.

Edwards devoted himself to these people. Over and over again in his pastoral career, he laid out the beauty of conversion and the goodness of the Christian life, displaying with intricate reasoning, eloquent speech, and personal ardor the glories of biblical faith. He was not unlike the two Israelite spies who first glimpsed the Promised Land and rushed back to tell the people of their findings. After they told the Israelites of the earthly paradise that awaited them, the people rejected their counsel, stunning the spies, who knew that no good reason existed to avoid entering the land prepared for them by God (Joshua 1–6). In his day, many centuries later, Edwards strove to do the same by educating his people about the good life and its ultimate end, heaven. Lackluster effort on the part of his hearers frustrated his good purposes, but he never stopped sharing the good news of the land to come.

The Free Offer of the Good Life

A key part of Edwards's doctrine of the good life was its accessibility. The "saving evidence of the truth of the gospel," proclaimed the preacher in "A Divine and Supernatural Light":

IS ATTAINABLE BY PERSONS of mean capacities, and advantages, as well as those that are of the greatest parts and learning. If the evidence of the gospel depended only on history, and such reasonings as learned men only are capable of, it would be above the reach of far the greatest part of mankind. But persons, with but an ordinary degree of knowledge, are capable, without a long and subtile train of reasoning, to see the divine excellency of the things of religion: they are capable of being taught by the Spirit of God, as well as learned men. The evidence that is this way obtained, is vastly better and more satisfying, than all that can be obtained by the arguings of those that are most learned, and greatest masters of reason. And babes are as capable of knowing these things, as the wise and prudent; and they are often hid from these, when they are revealed to those; 1 Corinthians 1:26–27, "For ye see your calling,

brethren, how that not many wise men, after the flesh, not
many mighty, not many noble, are called. But God hath
chosen the foolish things of the world . . ." (*Works* 17, 423)

One did not taste the goodness of God only when possessing
extreme intelligence or seasoned maturity. Any person at any
time in any situation could "see the divine excellency of the
things of religion." Children, mere "babes," Edwards noted,
"are as capable of knowing these things, as the wise and prudent." Edwards assured his people that the good life was free
to all and immensely beneficial. The unhappy had only to act
in their best interests to experience the joy of Christianity.
The hungry had only to direct their appetites to the sweetest
delights on earth to taste the goodness of God. The good life's
excellency is matched only by its sensible nature. It is not only
the best way of life, it is the most sensible, fitting perfectly
with common sense and self-preservation.

How the Bible Discloses the Good Life

The Lord had not made the good life hard to find, but had
disclosed its character in the Bible. Edwards sought to illuminate what the Scripture set forth on this important subject
and to avoid moralistic views of the divine text. In a sermon
entitled "The Importance and Advantage of a Thorough
Knowledge of Divine Truth," Edwards suggested that the
Bible gives us the only sure means to happiness in this world:

BUT WE WHO ENJOY the light of the gospel are more happy; we are not left, as to this particular, in the dark. God hath told us about what things we should chiefly employ our understandings, having given us a book full of divine instructions, holding forth many glorious objects about which all rational creatures should chiefly employ their understandings. These instructions are accommodated to persons of all capacities and conditions, and proper to be studied, not only by men of learning, but by persons of all capacities and conditions, and proper to be studied, not only by men of learning, but by persons of every charac-ter, learned and unlearned, young and old, men and women. Therefore the acquisition of knowledge in these things should be a main business of all those who have the advantage of enjoying the holy Scriptures. (*Works* 22, 35)

The Bible was no mere collection of heady maxims to Edwards. It was "full of divine instructions" and "glorious objects" that "persons of all capacities and conditions" needed to make their "main business." The truth, argued the theolo-gian, enlightened the mind and brought it out of "the dark," leaving Christians "more happy" than anyone else. Though Edwards gave considerable priority to the emotions, he believed that joy sprung from knowledge of the truth. Such thinking defies much popular thought of our modern age, in which many people place emotion or the pursuit of sensory pleasure before truth. For this reason many people live in a kind of dissonance, experiencing a lifestyle of constant tension and frustration, their actions never agreeing with their minds, their desires constantly pushing them to ignore their consciences and the innate knowledge of what is right. Edwards shows us that in order to live joyfully, we must first let truth grip and renew us. Only then will we apprehend the true nature of the text and find faith to defeat our doubts about the Word.

Edwards believed that the Bible both creates the good life and sustains it. In his view, expressed in "The Importance and Advantage of a Thorough Knowledge of Divine Truth," God had spring-loaded the content of the Bible with power to transform lives and fill them with fresh delight.

THE THINGS OF DIVINITY are things of superlative excellency, and are worthy that all should make a business of endeavoring to grow in the knowledge of them. There are no things so worthy to be known as these things. They are as much above those things which are treated of in other sciences, as heaven is above the earth. God himself, the eternal Three in One, is the chief object of this science, in the next place, Jesus Christ, as God-man and Mediator, and the glorious work of redemption, the most glorious work that ever was wrought, then the great things of the heavenly world, the glorious and eternal inheritance purchased by Christ, and promised in the gospel; the work of the Holy

Spirit of God on the hearts of men; our duty to God, and
the way in which we ourselves may become like angels,
and like God himself in our measure: all these are objects
of this science. (*Works* 22, 35)

One's happiness in these things depended only on how much
time and attention one gave to the Word, counseled the
pastor:

THE MORE YOU HAVE of a rational knowledge of the
things of the gospel, the more opportunity will there be,
when the Spirit shall be breathed into your heart, to see
the excellency of these things, and to taste the sweetness of
them. The heathens, who have no rational knowledge of
the things of the gospel, have no opportunity to see the
excellency of them; and therefore the more rational knowledge of these things you have, the more opportunity and
advantage you have to see the divine excellency and glory
of them. (*Works* 22, 100)

Time in the Word brought one to a "rational knowledge" of
the gospel, which if converted to practice would furnish certain proof of the truth of Christianity, according to Edwards's
sermon "A Divine and Supernatural Light":

A TRUE SENSE OF THE DIVINE excellency of the things of
God's Word doth more directly and immediately convince

of the truth of them; and that because the excellency of these things is so superlative. There is a beauty in them that is so divine and godlike, that is greatly and evidently distinguishing of them from things merely human, or that men are the inventors and authors of; a glory that is so high and great, that when clearly seen, commands assent to their divinity, and reality. When there is an actual and lively discovery of this beauty and excellency, it won't allow of any such thought as that it is an human work, or the fruit of men's invention. This evidence, that they, that are spiritually enlightened, have of the truth of the things of religion, is a kind of intuitive and immediate evidence. They believe the doctrines of God's Word to be divine, because they see divinity in them, i.e. they see a divine, and transcendent, and most evidently distinguishing glory in them; such a glory as, if clearly seen, don't leave room to doubt of their being of God, and not of men. (*Works* 17, 415)

Edwards's view of the Bible and its truths challenges superficial evangelical views of God's Word. So many of us struggle to even open the Bible, let alone allow it to transform our lives and shatter our nagging doubts. The Northampton theologian propels us out of a scriptural formalism, a mindset that perceives the Bible as dry and dusty, and into one that recognizes the "divine and godlike" beauty of the Bible and its "transcendent" glory. These attributes render the Word a text that "commands assent," that grips us with a sovereign force and lifts us up out of listlessness and boredom to contemplate the holy realities of God and His work.

Word and Spirit Birth Powerful Faith

Edwards's electric view of conversion stemmed from a catalytic understanding of the Bible, as one can see. Little wonder that his own spiritual life and ministry generated so much heat and light. How one views the Word of God and interacts with it clearly plays a significant role in how one understands conversion and the life it creates. A big view of God, the Bible, and the Christian life brings deep faith and happiness; a shallow view of God, the Bible, and the Christian life creates shallow faith and malnourished happiness. The Bible creates faith through the work of the Spirit, and the Bible sustains and deepens faith as the Christian allows it to permeate his life.

While studying the natural world was engaging, believers found in the Bible a "knowledge" that "is above all others sweet and joyful." In "A Divine and Supernatural Light" he mused that:

> MEN HAVE A GREAT DEAL of pleasure in human knowl-
> edge, in studies of natural things; but this is nothing to that
> joy which arises from this divine light shining into the soul.
> This light gives a view of those things that are immensely
> the most exquisitely beautiful, and capable of delighting

the eye of the understanding. This spiritual light is the
dawning of the light of glory in the heart. There is nothing
so powerful as this to support persons in affliction, and to
give the mind peace and brightness, in this stormy and
dark world. (*Works* 17, 424)

Many people, including some Christian people, panic and
lose hope when they encounter the afflictions and trials that
come to us all. How tragic that this is so, for as Edwards
pointed out, God has given all believers a "divine light shining
into the soul" that will "support persons in affliction" and regularly "give the mind peace and brightness, in this stormy and
dark world." To illustrate, Edwards pointed to the innumer-
able believers in history who had borne up under incredible
hardship due to their intimate connection to the God of the
Bible. He memorialized these people in his sermon "The Reality of Conversion," even as he urged his own flock to emulate
their examples:

BUT MANY THOUSANDS—yea, and millions—of professing Christians that have had this trial have acquitted themselves so under it as to give the most remarkable evidences
of a supernatural love to God and weanedness from the
world, for they have been tried with the most extreme sufferings and cruel tortures that man could invent. And the
sufferings of many of them have been lengthened out to a
very great length. Their persecutors have kept 'em under

trying torments that, if possible, they might conquer them
by wearing out of their spirits. But they have rather chosen
to undergo all and have held out in suffering unto the
death rather than deny Christ. Such has been their faith
and their love and their courage that their enemies could
not by any means overcome it, though they had 'em in
their hands to execute their will upon them. And very often
have they suffered all with the greatest composedness of
spirit, yea, and with cheerfulness. And many of them have
appeared exceeding joyful under their torments and have
glorified in tribulation.

The pastor continued his dramatic argument, seeking to
inspire his congregation to stronger, deeper, thicker faith:

AND THUS IT HAS BEEN not only with some few persons—
or with here and there an exempt instance—that have
braved it out through an extraordinary stoutness and
ruggedness of spirit; but so it has been with multitudes of
all sort: many that have been under the decays of old age,
long after the strength of nature has begun to fail and they
were in that state wherein are wont very much to lose their
natural courage; and also in women and even children and
persons of a delicate and weak constitution. Such as these
have, by their faith and love to Christ and courage in his
cause, conquered the greatest and cruelest monarchs of the

earth. In all the most dreadful things that their power could inflict upon them, they have rather chosen to suffer afflic-tion than in the least to depart from their dear Lord and Savior." (Kimnach, 87–88)

As one can see from this material, Edwards believed the "taste," the hunger for God given by the Spirit, changed the way a person understood themselves and their mission. The taste for the good life—the cruciform, Christ-centered, self-denying life—caused people to take on "an extraordinary stoutness and ruggedness of spirit," to power through a "delicate and weak constitution," and all manner of "dreadful things" in order to show "their faith and love to Christ." The pastor, as one can see, did not equate the good life with the easy life. Indeed, becoming a Christian often makes one's life harder, as Christ's own teachings show (see Matthew 5:2–12, for example). Yet even in the midst of bitter suffering brought on by Christian faith, believers tasted a spiritual sweetness that transcended all else. Clinging to Christ could have dramatic, even deadly, consequences, but even these did not deter many Christians from living boldly in the world, standing up for the Savior before "the greatest and cruelest monarchs of the earth."

As Edwards showed, the "taste" for spiritual things pro-duced an unmistakably original way of life. The conversion of a sinner did not involve a subduing of the heart or a dulling of the mind. When a person came to living faith in the living Christ, they came alive. Others around them *seemed* alive, seemed to have it all as they pursued their natural appetites and gratified their inherent desires. But the Christian alone is truly happy, having discovered the taste, the undeniable passion, for the things of God, which alone can satisfy the heart of mankind forever. Only this fact explained the otherwise ordinary men and women throughout history who exchanged the temporal things of this life for the supernatural pleasures of overcoming, joyful, Spirit-filled faith.

Tasting the Good Life

The world is complicated now. Thousands of paths present themselves to us, all offering a form of salvation or a type of promised transcendence. As we observe where these paths lead, however, one sees that so many do not satisfy. The movie star with all the wealth and looks and attention overdoses on drugs. The politician with tremendous influence squanders it for a tryst. The spiritually enlightened seeker following mystic paths grows disillusioned when suffering punches a hole in her worldview. Over and over again, these stories play out, all with the same ultimate ending: the natural affections, driven by sin, do not lead to lasting happiness, but to a wilderness of confusion and pain.

Only one path, one way, one life, offers us eternity and eternal happiness. "There is no kind of love in the world," wrote Edwards, "that has had such great, visible effects in men as love to Christ has had, though he be an unseen object, which [is] an evidence of a divine work in the hearts of men, infusing that love into them" (Kimnach, 89). The "divine work," the taste for Christ, shows us the way to God. Scripture reminds us that "There is a way that seems right to a man, but its end is the way to death" (Proverbs 14:12). This is the inevitable end of following our natural passions. But those who have been reborn by the Spirit will taste the good life given us by a great God.

Living the Good Life

Master Your Tastes

*T*he Holy Spirit creates a taste in the Christian for God and the things of God (see Romans 12). This renewing work, however, does not altogether eradicate our taste for the things of the world. Though saved, we must do battle on a daily basis with our natural predilection for sin.

We must do so in a personal way, based on our own specific struggles. If we have a weakness for pornography and lust, we must pray and work for mastery over this sin and seek to heal or change what is distorted. If we yearn for possessions, we must redirect our hunger toward the things of God, and push that same energy toward storing up treasures in heaven (Matthew 6:20). If we live selfishly, we must free ourselves from this trap by adopting a generous, others-centered way of life. In these and many other areas, we need to follow an Edwardsean way of life and rightly channel our passions and appetites. We do not need to eradicate or destroy them, but to direct them to holy things, to patterns of living that please the Lord.

It will be very helpful for Christians to join a church, get involved with a small group, and pursue discipleship with a pastor, elder, or mature Christian. These people will help us to see the sins that we personally struggle with and will help us to devise a plan for holiness that involves saturation in the Word and accountability to the local church. God has made us for fellowship; He has made us for the church. We will find encouragement, accountability, and the means to joyful growth in churches engulfed by the Word that possess a vision for the good life.

Seek the Sweetness of Christ

*W*e need to seek the sweetness of Christ. This goes hand-in-hand with mastering our appetites. As we seek to orient our lives to God's design, we need to consciously focus on the sweetness of Jesus Christ, our Savior (Psalm 45 will help us greatly here). On a daily basis, we need to thank our Father for sending His Son to die in our place, exchanging our depravity for His righteousness. This should be a part of our prayer to begin the day. The more we think about and meditate on Christ and His work, the sweeter it will become to us. The luster of the world's pleasures will fade as the light of Christ rises in our hearts. Let us place Christ at the center of our thoughts. We are united to Him by the Spirit and are living a resurrection life because of Him. How important, then, that we seek to experience and taste the sweetness of this reality on a daily basis.

Know the Power of the Word

*T*he Bible, as Edwards shows us, is filled with the highest, best things of God. It is not, contrary to what some say, a collection of inspired teachings, pithy moralisms, or life lessons. It is a transformative book. It is the mind and heart of God communicated to the mind and heart of man (2 Peter 1:21). It produces the faith that so many of us thirst for and find elusive. It never leaves us empty; it never fails to encourage or teach; it never ceases to satisfy. Though a book, it is filled with infinite wisdom and beauty (see Psalm 119 for celebration of this truth). If we would experience the glory of biblical Christianity, we need to devote ourselves to studying and breathing in the Bible. It will purify us, cleanse us, give us an appetite for holy things, diminish our hunger for worldly things. The Bible is a powerful book. We need to read it often —not to check off a holiness box, but to come into direct contact with the Lord of heaven and earth.

We will be greatly helped in this end if we fellowship at a church that believes that the Word is powerful and embodies this belief in its life and mission. We need far fewer gurus and practitioners who concentrate on methods and schemes and far more sages and pastor-theologians who, in an Edwardsean fashion, prepare a feast from the Word each week for their congregation. How many of our preachers produce sermons that, like Edwards's, someone will find provocative, powerful, and eye-opening over 250 years later?

In whatever way we can, whether big or small, we need to encourage the development of this kind of pastor, who will offer the people of God nothing less and nothing more than the breath of God, the Holy Bible, in all its majesty and glory. We should talk to our pastors about how we can contribute in big and small ways to such an important movement.

Leave a Legacy of Faith

We are reminded as we read Edwards's testimony of past Christians that we ourselves will soon leave this world. We are faced now with the opportunity to leave a legacy of faith. It is not only pastoral leaders like Edwards who may author a story of faith, perseverance, and triumph. Every Christian—every single believer—may in their own way offer those who come behind a picture of faithful, vibrant Christianity. The janitor who works with joy to the glory of God; the grandmother who prays constantly for her family from a nursing home bed; the professor who disciples his students and cares for them long after they leave school; the auto mechanic who regularly witnesses to his fellow workers in the garage; the athlete who gives glory to God in good seasons and bad— all of these people and many more may in their particular place and time leave a legacy. We should desire that our families, most of all, would testify to our faith and godliness and that our children, as with the Proverbs 31 woman, would rise up and call us blessed when we have left this earth. Each of us has the opportunity to be such a Christian, a salt-and-light Christian, who leaves his peers and friends with a "taste" of something divine, a living witness to a greater reality.

CHAPTER FOUR

The Pleasures of the Good Life

*H*ow do you like your religion? Light? Rules-based? Mystery-infused? Do you prefer it to be fun, or sober? Do you like structure, or do you prefer freedom?

Perhaps we should narrow this line of questioning a bit. How do you like your gospel? Full and rich, pervading all areas of life? Or light and airy, salvific in the end, but requiring little commitment in the meantime?

The question is cheeky. But, sadly, it also seems to represent the thinking of some corners of the evangelical world. Immersed in a commercialistic, pragmatic, self-serving culture, many of us approach faith and church like we approach the Starbucks counter. We select the components of biblical religion that we prefer, leave the rest on the menu, and go on our merry way, oblivious to how our culture has molded us into consumerist Christians. If we can reduce this attitude to its fundamental problem, we might say that it suffers from a diminished view of Christian faith. Or, to put it another way, it suffers from a small gospel, a weak gospel, a gospel that's easily forgotten.

What does this mean, though? What is a "small gospel?" A small gospel is a spiritually limited gospel. It can *tweak* aspects of a person's life, but it is largely unable to *transform*. It speaks to one's sins and habits, yes, but only softly, never forcefully. It cajoles, and occasionally threatens, but like an ineffectual parent, only rarely achieves its will. When it comes to the suffering of this world, the deep trials, it tries to comfort and console, but can do so with only limited effect, leaving the hurting soul with the theological equivalent of some nice words and a tissue. It is well-intentioned but ultimately ineffective.

This gospel, malnourished and unimpressive, stands in contrast with the bold message of the Bible preached by a flood of preachers throughout history—Athanasius, Augustine, Luther, Calvin, Wesley, Whitefield, and Jonathan Edwards. For his part, Edwards bore into the Bible his entire life, spending hour upon hour plumbing its depths and offering his people the richest doctrine he could. In going directly to the text, Edwards found not a small gospel, but a large one. This large gospel promised not to chip away at the human heart, but to overhaul it, performing a kind of spiritual quadruple bypass so that sinners who once muddled along could experience the power and joy of the good life.

Though he spelled out the transforming effects of the biblical message in countless sermons, Edwards preached five in particular that extol the virtues of the Christian in particularly affective ways: "The Spiritual Blessings of the Gospel Represented by a Feast," "Christ is to the Heart Like a Tree Planted by a River," "Love the Sum of All Virtue," "Divine Love Alone Lasts Eternally," and "The Peace Which Christ Gives His True Followers." These sermons lay out sensory pleasures—feasting, drinking, peace—that in unique and moving ways show the depth of the *evangel* and the contours of the good life it creates. In these messages, we see that it is not a small-sized faith, neatly compartmentalized, that makes for the happiest existence, but a large, pervasive, scriptural gospel that conquers our sin, satisfies our hearts, and allows us to live the good life prepared for us by God Himself.

The Gospel Feast

In his sermon "The Spiritual Blessings of the Gospel Represented by a Feast," Edwards used the imagery of a harvest meal to illustrate the bounty of blessings that the gospel bestowed on the Christian. In our day, we are less acquainted with feasts, but in the eighteenth century, such a meal represented a grand occasion, a time of celebration, in which one forgot one's cares and shared food and happiness with friends and family. "In this feast," said the pastor:

God is the host; 'tis he that makes the provision and invites the guests. And sinners are the invited guests. Believers are those that accept of the invitation. And Jesus Christ, with his benefits that he purchased by his obedience and death, and which he communicates by his Spirit, is the entertainment. This is the meat and drink. Christ gives himself for the life of the world. He is slain that we may as it were eat his flesh and drink his blood, as the sacrifices of old were slain and then that which was not burnt was eaten. Thus considered, God the Father is the host and Christ is the entertainment. Believers, as they live a life of faith, they do as it were feed upon Christ Jesus; they live upon him; he is their daily bread. (*Works* 14, 281–2)

God invites His guests, who have done nothing to deserve their place at the table. The "entertainment," or the center of the occasion, is "Jesus Christ, with his benefits that he purchased by his obedience and death." Edwards intended the picture this metaphor created to be a sensory one, reminding his hearers in a tangible way of the nearness and goodness of God.

Every feast comes at a cost, but no celebration came at a greater cost than did the gospel feast. God, Edwards noted, paid dearly for His people to dine with Him:

AS FEASTS ARE EXPENSIVE and are provided at the expense of the host, so the provision which God has in the gospel made for our souls be exceeding expensive unto [him]. We have it for nothing. It costs us nothing, but it cost God a great deal. Fallen men can't be feasted but at vast expense. We are by sin sunk infinitely low, into the lowest depths of misery and want, and our famishing souls could not be provided for [but] under infinite expense. All that we have from God for the salvation and support and nourishment of our souls cost exceeding dear. Never were any that were feasted at so dear a rate as believers: what they eat and drink is a thousand times more costly than what they eat at the tables [of] princes, that is far-fetched and dear bought.

The pastor continued:

EVERY CRUMB OF BREAD that they eat and every drop of wine that they drink is more costly than so much gold or gems. God purchased it at no less a rate than with the blood of his only and infinitely dear Son. That holiness and that favor, and that peace and joy which they have, it was bought with the heart's blood of the Son of God, his precious life. He made his soul an offering. Christ Jesus obtained this provision by victory. He was obliged to fight for it as it were up to his knees in blood that he might obtain it; yea, he waded through a sea of blood to get it for us. (*Works* 14, 282–83)

Salvation did not come cheaply. Before he unfolded the glories of the Christian life, Edwards took pains to show his people that their salvation, their place at the table, cost the Father His Son and the Son His life. Though so many of us covet the finer things of life, which come at a great cost, the gospel feast that the saved enjoy "is a thousand times more costly than what they eat at the tables [of] princes," who spread the most lavish meals in all the world. "Holiness," "favor," "peace and joy," all these Christ gave His people in infinite amount. But He did not simply wave a wand to make this happen; "he waded through a sea of blood" to bless us. Contrary to the light and airy prosperity teachings of some preachers today, which often touch briefly on the gospel while majoring on the supposed wealth that it brings, Edwards anchored His understanding of the blessings of the good life in the atoning death of Christ, the price of salvation that only divinity could pay.

The Food Spread Before Us in the Feast

Having compared salvation to a great feast, Edwards considered the character of its offerings. What, exactly, does the immense gospel of the Bible do in the lives of those who believe it?:

THE GRACE OF CHRIST JESUS, it nourishes the soul; it gives life and strength to it. Before the soul receives this grace, it is dead. In this it doth more than bread does to the body, that does but preserve the life of the body and revives it when weakened and languishing; but this heavenly food revives men when dead. And it also continues the life of the soul: the soul, after it is revived, would die again, were it not for the continuance of supply of grace and spiritual nourishment. It strengthens the soul as food does the body. The soul in its natural condition is a poor, feeble, languishing thing, having no strength; but the grace of Christ makes it strong and vigorous. And this spiritual nourishment makes the soul to grow, as food doth the body. The supplies of the Spirit of God increase the life and vigor of the soul, increases the understanding, increases holy inclinations and affections; as bodily nourishment increases all the members of the body, makes a proportionable growth of every part. (*Works* 14, 284)

The gospel of Christ works in the heart to spiritually enrich it and saturate it with the sweet things of God. It is not a weak message, a pleasant but powerless story. It "revives men when dead," it "nourishes the soul," giving "life and strength to it," rendering it "strong and vigorous" in the things of the Lord. As we feed on divine grace, "this spiritual nourishment makes the soul to grow" just like food does "the body." "Every part" of our being, including our "understanding" and our "holy inclinations and affections," grows and flourishes and bursts with life due to the gospel. One cannot fully comprehend its effects. It is too great a message, too powerful a reality, to fully understand and appreciate. So said the pastor in another section of "The Spiritual Blessings":

> THERE IS EVERY KIND OF THING dispensed in Christ that tends to make us excellent and amiable, and every kind of thing that tends to make us happy. There is that which shall fill every faculty of the soul and in a great variety. What a glorious variety is there for the entertainment of the understanding! How many glorious objects set forth, most worthy to be meditated upon and understood! There are all the glorious attributes of God and the beauties of Jesus Christ, and manifold wonders to be seen in the way of salvation, the glories of heaven and the excellency of Christian graces. And there is a glorious variety for the satisfying the will: there are pleasures, riches and honors; there are all things desirable or lovely. There is various entertainment for the affections, for love, for joy, for desire and hope. The blessings are innumerable. (*Works* 14, 285–86)

Edwards's God-soaked conception of the delights of Christianity soars past our reductionistic, narcissistic, Christianity-in-a-box kind of faith. As he saw things, life is not about us and the achievement of our own frequently shallow ideals and hopes. Those who possess faith in the gospel gain a connection to the Lord of the universe, who bursts with "glorious attributes." Like a feast that features every kind of food possible, Christians have "every kind of thing" through Christ "that tends to make us excellent and amiable" and "happy." Love, joy, peace, comfort, hope, grace, forgiveness, mercy, happiness, confidence—all these and a thousand other blessings are ours, flowing to us in "inexhaustible plenty" like "rivers of pleasure forevermore." This is what the good life looks like: more blessing than we can quantify in more areas than we can identify.

Christian Living Is Fundamentally Joyful Living

Because of the constant availability of all these good things, the Christian life was a joyful one. Edwards closed his sermon with words summarizing this point:

FEASTS ARE MADE upon joyful occasions and for the manifestations of joy. Ecclesiastes 10:19, "A feast is made for laughter." Christians, in the participation and communion of gospel benefits, have joy unspeakable and full of glory, a sweeter delight than any this world affords. We are invited in that forecited place, Isaiah 55:1–2, to come, that our souls may delight themselves in fatness. When the prodigal son returned, they killed the fatted calf and made a feast, and sang and danced and made merry; which represents the joy there [is] in a sinner, and concerning him, when he comes to Christ. (*Works* 14, 287)

The fundamental reality of the Christian life was joy in the pastor's eyes. Not rigidity, not ecstasy, not sobriety, not gloominess, not emotional stasis. Because the Savior has substituted Himself for sinners, and has returned triumphant from the grave, so too may sinners return to life, and taste for all their lives "joy unspeakable and full of glory," that which is "a sweeter delight than any this world affords." This does not deny real pain and real suffering, of course. But it reflects that the goodness of God so pervades the Christian life that nothing—not *anything*—can rob a Christian of the delights of the gospel. For all our lives, we eat at a full table, and eat a rich feast, with Christ the head of all. The good life is a feast.

A Vision of Divine Love

Though Edwards often elaborated on the fruits of the gospel, he rarely provided richer fare for his congregation than he did on the specific subjects of love and peace—spiritual principles given the children of God by the indwelling Spirit in the moment when the redeemed first tasted the sweetness of Christ. In his sermons "Love the Sum of All Virtue" and "Divine Love Alone Lasts Eternally," the Northampton theologian discussed the love given to believers by God. In the first sermon, he covered the flow of this love from the center of the Godhead to the heart of the Christian. In the gospel, he argued:

THERE IT IS REVEALED how the Father and the Son are one in love, that we might be induced in like manner to be one with them, and with one another, agreeable to Christ's prayer, John 17:21–23, "That they all may be one; as thou Father art in me and I in thee, that they also may be one in us; that the world may believe that thou hast sent me. And the glory which thou gavest me I have given them; that they may be one, even as we are one; I in them, and thou in me, that they may be made perfect in one; and that the world may know that thou hast sent me, and hast loved them, as thou hast loved me." The gospel teaches us the doctrine of the eternal electing love of God, and reveals how God loved those that are redeemed by Christ before the foundation of the world; and how he then gave them to the Son, and the Son loved them as his own. . . . The gospel reveals such love as nothing else reveals. John 15:13, "Greater love hath no man than this." Romans 5:7–8, "Scarcely for a righteous man will one die; yet peradventure for a good man some would even dare to die. But God commendeth his love towards us, in that while we were yet sinners, Christ died for us." God and Christ in the gospel revelation appear as clothed with love, as being as it were on a throne of mercy and grace, a seat of love encompassed about with pleasant beams of love. Love is the light and glory which are about the throne on which God sits. (*Works* 8, 144–45)

The root of the love that Christians experience is the love shared by the members of the Trinity. To rightly understand the biblical notion of love according to Edwards, one had to first realize that the object of God's love was the Godhead. The members of the Trinity, the Father, Son, and Holy Spirit, exist in perfect harmony together, constantly sharing delight in their relationships with one another. From the overflow of this love came the offer of the Father and Son "to be one with them, and with one another." This association came through the "eternal electing love of God" that commissioned the redeeming work of the Son.

This section enriches our understanding of Christian love, as it shows us the deeply God-centered nature of the love we experience and reveals that we cannot claim pride of place in the eyes of the Father. The Father has loved us, yes, but He has loved us in the death of His Son. We see, then, that all of the blessings we experience in this life, including the love of God, come to us from the overflow of the love of the Trinity. The good life proceeds from the outflow of the love shared by the Father, Son, and Holy Spirit. Only then can we apprehend a right understanding of ourselves and a biblical definition of love. Only then will the gospel sparkle in our minds with an "exceeding sweet and pleasant light, pleasant like the beautiful colors of the rainbow," a message with greater depth than any mind could conceive.

The Eternal Nature of Divine Love

The Northampton theologian concentrated on the effect of this love in the experience of the Christian in his sermon "Divine Love Alone Lasts Eternally." He connected this love with the work of the Holy Spirit, building on his belief that the character or identity of the Spirit is love:

> THAT DIVINE LOVE is that great fruit of the Spirit of Christ which never fails, and in which his continued and ever-lasting influence and indwelling in his church appears. You have heard that the Spirit of Christ is forever given to the church of Christ, or given that it may dwell in his church and people forever in influences which shall never fail. And therefore however many fruits of the Spirit may be but temporary, and have their periods in which they fail, yet it must be so that there must be some way of influence, and some kind of fruit of the Spirit, which is unfailing and ever-lasting. And this, even divine or Christian love, is that fruit in the communicating and maintaining and exercising of which his unfailing, eternal influences appear. This is a fruit of the Spirit which never fails or ceases in the church of Christ, whether we consider the church with respect to its particular members, or whether we consider it as a collective body. (*Works* 8, 356)

Edwards reminds the believer that the Spirit "never fails" and exercises a "continued and everlasting influence" on the children of God, bearing "fruit" in which "his unfailing, eternal influences appear." Love, in its fullest and most biblical sense, comes from God, emanating from heaven like a transmission from another world. The Spirit, our indwelling spiritual radar, allows us to receive this call, to see for the first time love in its truest form, and to receive it. Having picked up this signal, we send it back to God, and the cycle continues, love between God and Christian never ceasing.

As one can readily see, divine love is not weak. It is tough, and strong, and enables us to persevere. Once we have received the Spirit, the endowment of divine love, we find strength to transcend our difficulties and defeat our enemies:

> IF WE CONSIDER THE CHURCH of Christ [individually], or with respect to the particular members of which it consists, divine love is an unfailing fruit of the Spirit. Every one of the true members of Christ's invisible church are possessed of this fruit of the Spirit in their hearts. Divine or Christian love is implanted there, and dwells there, and reigns there, and it is an everlasting fruit of the Spirit. It never fails; it never fails in this world, but remains through all trials and opposition. Romans 8:35–37, "Who shall separate us from the love of Christ? Shall tribulation, or distress, or persecution, or famine, or nakedness, or peril, or sword? As it is written, for thy sake we are killed all the day long; we are

accounted as sheep for the slaughter. Nay, in all these things
we are more than conquerors through him that loved us."
(*Works* 8, 358)

Because of its triumphant nature, Edwards believed that love
represents the greatest gift of any the Father could give. He
elaborated on this point:

THIS DOCTRINE TEACHES US how greatly such influence
and fruits of the Spirit working grace in the heart, sum-
marily consisting in Christian and divine love, are to be
valued. It is the design of the Apostle to teach us this by
showing how charity never fails, though all other gifts and
fruits of the Spirit fail. This is the most excellent fruit of the
Spirit, without which the best extraordinary and miraculous gifts are nothing. This is the end of which they are the
means, and which is more excellent than the means. Let us
therefore earnestly seek this blessed fruit of the Spirit; and
let us seek that it may abound in our hearts, that the love
of God may more and more be shed abroad in our hearts,
and that we may love the Lord Jesus Christ in sincerity, and
love one another as Christ hath loved us. Hereby we shall
possess that which never fails. We shall have that within us
which will be of an immortal nature, and which will be a
sure evidence of our own blessed immortality, and the
beginning of eternal life in our souls. (*Works* 8, 365)

Edwards extolled all the gifts and fruits of the Spirit, but he
made clear that love was "the most excellent." Without it, "the
best extraordinary and miraculous gifts are nothing." Divine
affection planted in the heart is nothing less than "the beginning of eternal life in our souls." The gospel as Edwards saw
it was not small. It was great. It brought God's love to sinful,
loveless, afflicted hearts, and gave them an "immortal nature."
Love was the planted seed of God, given in this life, which
would grow up in the next to maturity and fullness. That
which the human heart seeks in so many forms, whether
romantic, parental, physical, affectional, or any other, that
which it searches the world to find, is located in the gospel,
the special communication of God's love to His creation. The
good life is found in the gospel.

A Vision of Divine Peace

A second major effect of the gospel involved peace of a
decidedly otherworldly kind. In his sermon "The Peace Which
Christ Gives His True Followers," Edwards illuminated the
nature of divine peace, identifying it as a product of faith in
the gospel. He began by discussing Christ's personal gift of
peace to His children:

> IT WAS HIS PEACE that he gave them; as it was the same
> kind of peace which he himself enjoyed. The same excellent
> and divine peace which he ever had in God; and which he
> was about to receive in his exalted state in a vastly greater

perfection and fullness: for the happiness Christ gives to his people, is a participation of his own happiness: agreeable to what Christ says in this same dying discourse of his, John 15:11, "These things have I said unto you, that my joy might remain in you." And in his prayer that he made with his disciples at the conclusion of this discourse; John 17:13, "And now come I unto thee, and these things I speak in the world, that they might have my joy fulfilled in themselves." And John 17:22, "And the glory which thou gavest me, I have given them." (*Works* 25, 539)

Along with providing His people security and hope, the peace He purchased through death brought reconciliation to all of man's relationships—to God, to others, and with himself:

OUR LORD JESUS CHRIST has bequeathed true peace and comfort to his followers. Christ is called the "prince of peace" (Isaiah 9:6). And when he was born into the world, the angels on that joyful and wonderful occasion sang "Glory to God in the highest, on earth peace"; because of that peace which he should procure for and bestow on the children of men; peace with God, and peace one with another, and tranquility and peace within themselves: which last is especially the benefit spoken of in the text. This Christ has procured for his followers and laid a foundation for their enjoyment of, in that he has procured for them the other two, viz.: peace with God, and one with another. He has procured for them peace and reconciliation with God, and his favor and friendship, in that he satisfied for their sins, and laid a foundation for the perfect removal of the guilt of sin, and the forgiveness of all their trespasses, and wrought out for them a perfect and glorious righteousness, most acceptable to God and sufficient to recommend them to God's full acceptance and to the adoption of children, and to the eternal fruits of his fatherly kindness. (*Works* 25, 542)

Those who seek unbroken peace in the world outside of Christianity do not know that no other foundation for harmony and security exists. Lasting comfort is found not in a system, an ideology, or even a galvanizing figure, but only in the God-man, Jesus Christ. He *is* peace. Through His death and resurrection on behalf of His people, "He has procured for them peace and reconciliation with God," the ultimate need of all who live. While on earth, we seek and pray for peace, but we do so knowing that whatever treaty is agreed to, whatever truce is brokered, it is earthly and cannot ultimately last. With Edwards, we must affirm that only Christ and the "perfect and glorious righteousness" He gives can meet our needs and calm our hearts. The good life is a life of peace.

Peace's Practical Effects

The peace offered mankind in the gospel did not simply meet a general need of humanity, but through grace had a transformational effect on the heart of a regenerated sinner. The theologian suggested in "The Peace Which Christ Gives His True Followers" that:

GRACE TENDS TO TRANQUILITY, as it mortifies tumultuous desires and passions, subdues the eager and insatiable appetites of the sensual nature and greediness after the vanities of the world. It mortifies such principles as hatred, variance, emulation, wrath, envyings, and the like, which are a continual source of inward uneasiness and perturbation; and supplies those sweet, calming, and quieting principles of humility, meekness, resignation, patience, gentleness, forgiveness, and sweet reliance on God.

And it also tends to peace, as it fixes the aim of the soul to a certain end; so that the soul is no longer distracted and drawn contrary ways by opposite ends to be sought, and opposite portions to be obtained, and many masters of contrary wills and commands to be served; but the heart is fixed in the choice of one certain, sufficient, and unfailing good: and the soul's aim at this, and hope of it, is like an anchor to it that keeps it steadfast, that it should no more be driven to and fro by every wind. (*Works* 25, 544)

Here Edwards shows us how the grace of God given in the gospel quiets the frenetic heart. Grace, said the pastor, "mortifies tumultuous desires and passions, subdues the eager and insatiable appetites of the sensual nature," kills "hatred, variance, emulation, wrath, envyings," and "supplies those sweet, calming, and quieting principles" of a spiritual nature. The peace of the message of faith addresses head-on the natural restlessness and senseless destructiveness that characterize so many lost people. When the Spirit converts a sinner, He brings the heart to rest. This rest, Edwards contended, increases as one contemplates its presence:

BUT WITH RESPECT TO THE PEACE which Christ gives, reason is its great friend: the more that faculty is exercised, the more is it established; the more they consider and view things with truth and exactness, the firmer is their comfort and the higher their joy. How vast a difference is this, between [a Christian and a worldling]! How miserable are they who can't enjoy peace any otherwise than by hiding their eyes from the light and confining themselves to darkness, whose peace is properly stupidity: as the ease which a man has that has taken a dose of stupefying poison, and the ease and pleasure that a drunken man may have in an house on fire over his head, or the joy of a distracted man in thinking that he is a king, though a miserable wretch confined in Bedlam. Whereas, the peace that Christ gives

> to his true disciples is the light of life: something of the
> tranquility of heaven, the peace of the celestial paradise
> that has the glory of God to lighten it. (*Works* 25, 547–48)

The more one thinks of God's peace, and considers how much of it one possesses, the more one will experience it, says Edwards. Unlike the unbeliever, who hides from "consideration and reflection," the Christian counts "reason" his "great friend." This is a perceptive point. When we are lost, we do not like to acknowledge it. Instead, we fill our days with distractions, avoiding deep thought about our situations, choosing a constant stream of action over quiet moments of thought. The Christian, however, needs no such diversions. We are freed to evaluate our lives. We have been freed from pride and pretending, and from the peace that "is properly stupidity." As a result, we can live without fear.

Believers know that Christ has taken our burden from us, has forgiven us for all eternity, and has given us every blessing. We thus possess "something of the tranquility of heaven." In the same way that one easily spots unrest and fear in the unbeliever, one finds many Christians who radiate hope and calm trust in the Lord in all kinds of circumstances. Despite the deterioration of the body, the loss of a job, the death of a friend, Christians rooted in the gospel display otherworldly peace and trust, showing that the good life always yields good fruit.

Edwards closed his sermon by reminding his hearers of the eternal nature of the peace they possessed. His words

nicely close our study of the peace given to every follower of
the Lord as he invites us to marvel at the hope that is ours in
Christ:

I INVITE YOU NOW to a better portion; there are better
things provided for the sinful, miserable children of men.
There is a surer comfort and more durable peace: comfort
that you may enjoy in a state of safety, and on a sure foundation; a peace and rest that you may enjoy with reason
and with your eyes open; having all your sins forgiven,
your greatest and most aggravated transgressions blotted
out as a cloud, and buried as in the depths [of] the sea, that
they may be never found more: and being not only forgiven but accepted to favor, being the objects of God's com-
placence and delight, being taken into God's family and
made his child; and having good evidence that your name
was written on the heart of Christ before the world was
made, and an interest in that covenant of God that is
ordered in all things, and sure, wherein is promised no less
than life and immortality, an inheritance incorruptible and
undefiled, a crown of glory that fades not away: being in
such circumstances that nothing shall be able to prevent
your being happy to all eternity; having for the foundation
of your hope that love of God which is from eternity to
eternity; and his promise and oath, and his omnipotent

power, things infinitely firmer than mountains of brass. The
mountains shall depart and the hills be removed; yea, the
heavens shall vanish away like smoke, and the earth shall
wax old like a garment, yet these things will never be abol-
ished. (*Works* 25, 551)

The Bountiful Blessings of the Good Life

The love and peace of God—along with a multitude of
other blessings—are spread out before us like a feast. We have
only to seek them and we will find them. The goodness of
God is like the Lord Himself—vast and incomprehensible,
stretching beyond all that we can think or imagine. It proceeds from the sweetest message this world knows, the gospel
of Christ. As we have seen, the gospel is anything but small.
It is massive. It looms before us, offering to catapult us into
the realm of God where beauty and truth make their home.
Far from a personal preference or an arbitrary indulgence, the
gospel is the good news of God that claims our entire lives
and then floods them with more blessing than any worldview,
passion, or lifestyle we might consider. The gospel creates the
good life.

In this modern, self-centered, consumerist age, we need
to fasten ourselves to this biblical truth. We need to realize
that the gospel is great, engulfing every inch of our lives.
Viewed up close through the lens of Scripture, the good life
in Christ yields not a trickle, but an ocean of love and peace;
not a sampling of pleasures, but a feast of delights.

Living the Good Life

Enlarge Your Gospel Theologically

*T*he application in this chapter is quite simple. We need a fresh, new perspective on the gospel and its implications for all of life. Too many of us live according to a small, narrow gospel, an easily manageable faith that inflates when trials come and shrinks when sinful pleasures appear. This gospel has little ability to transform our hearts and minds and conform our thinking to the very thoughts of God. Small wonder that our lives so often look similar to those of unbelievers.

And how unsurprising that our joys are small, and our trials large. We do not have a faith that runs at a high enough horsepower to yield deep and lasting happiness in the things of God, or that can overpower and disarm the temptations and battles we face every day in a fallen world. We have little Scripture memorized to push us past despair and into comfort (Psalm 119:11). We are locked in patterns of sin that we never think to examine or ask another to evaluate. We spend a great deal of time and energy in worldly pursuits and almost none in fellowship with our brothers and sisters at church. We seek God's kingdom fourth or fifth rather than first. Thus, we have little deep joy, little pervasive happiness, and much turmoil and unhappiness.

The challenge, then, is to enlarge our gospel. We need to embrace the authority and majesty of God. We need to recognize His greatness and grandeur, His sovereignty and strength. We need to comprehend the depth of our sinfulness, and the magnitude of His love. We need to see the church as central to our faith and practice, and view it not as a religious club, a mere positive influence in the community, but a source of the very grace of God Almighty. We need theology of the most Edwardsean kind—bold, big, robust, and unswervingly in step with the Scripture and its portrait of the Lord. These are indispensable for living the good life in Christ. Our hearts are naturally proud, and resistant to authority, and we may have to wrestle with them to recognize the crystal-clear teachings of Scripture and their implications for our lives. This may be painful, but how much more pain will we experience in continuing to cling to a small gospel with little power that yields a life of small pleasures and great frustrations? If we want to taste the good life, the life infused with love and peace, we have to pursue it.

Understand True Love and Peace and Live Them Out

*A*s mentioned earlier in the chapter, health-and-wealth preachers have made quite a name for themselves. Prosperity theology is hot, and probably always will be, because it taps into the natural desire of the human heart for riches and comfort. This theology suffers from a deficient reading of Scripture, primarily. But it also suffers from a weak product.

Pastors of this stripe promise the nicest material goods this world affords, never knowing that the nicest car, the biggest house, the most exclusive address, the most stylish clothes, and the coolest technology all pale in comparison to the gifts the Lord waits to lavish upon His people. The Bible does not promise material wealth, it offers something far greater. It holds out the very riches of heaven, and invites all to come and enjoy them.

If you are a Christian, treasure the gifts you have. Do not abase them. Do not look over your shoulder at the fancy cars, the luxurious homes, the illicit sex shared by unbelievers (1 John 2:15). These are just passing things. They do not satisfy a person, ultimately, and even now they are not satisfying those who indulge in them. Only the Christian has true wealth. Only the Christian has true love, and true peace. Allow these attributes to course through you and fill you up with gratitude to the Father who ordained them and the Son who purchased them for you. Let them burst out in expression in your daily life (Matthew 6:19). As we have been shown love, and given peace, we need to share these gifts with the world. We need to love as we have been loved—expensively, sacrificially, graciously. We need to work for peace in this world wherever we can, just as God has made peace with us. By sharing the gospel and living it out through a mindset of mercy and justice, we fulfill this end, and attract others to join us in the glorious feast of abundant life that the Lord has provided.

Know the Relationship Between Grace and Peace

*W*e covered earlier Edwards's understanding of reconciliation between God and man, that is, how the Lord and His creation can find peace with one another. The doctrine of reconciliation through justification by faith illuminates how we conceive of our salvation and the very duties of our lives. As Edwards taught, we cannot obtain true and lasting peace by ourselves. This gift is given only by Christ, and it comes to us when the Spirit works in us to help us to understand how far away we are from God. Ironically, then, we can only be justified in God's sight and thereby reconciled to Him by realizing how bad we are and how great Christ's atonement is (Romans 5). This flies in the face of our instincts. We naturally wish to justify ourselves in God's sight by demonstrating our fitness for heaven. But in the biblical scheme, only those who lay down their pride and self-justification can find reconciliation with God.

Though we naturally want to try to make peace on our own terms, in laying down our lives and all our effort, we find fullness of joy. We find peace with God. Yet even after we do so, our sin rises up and threatens to condemn us. We feel that we are not worthy of God's grace and goodness, and we perhaps seek a way to prove our worth to God, to make peace anew. We forget that the Word teaches us that "where sin abounds, grace abounds" (Romans 5:20). It is never our effort that justifies us and brings peace with God. Though we are responsible to obey, the grace of God alone gives us peace with our Maker. Strange as it seems, God's goodness is magnified in the face of our weakness. As we follow Edwards and seek peace and blessing in our lives, and as we call others to salvation, we need to remember this central irony of the gospel.

CHAPTER FIVE

*The Shape of
the Good Life*

*T*here is a simple line that divides the happy from the unhappy in this world. The happy obey God; the unhappy disregard Him.

This seems a major reduction, a foible in reasoning. Examples abound of free spirits and liberated souls who give off the savor of happiness, who tune out and dial up, and find a certain zest of experience despite the difficulties of life. Popular culture certainly perpetuates this idea; the cinema and television abound with characters who buck the system, break the rules, and beat their own drum all the way to lasting satisfaction. Were one to seek a working philosophy of life based entirely on Hollywood, it seems likely that one would quickly learn to scorn rules, elevate personal determinism, and flout authority and tradition.

Many in the evangelical world resonate with this mindset. Desiring not to be tied down, many evangelicals downplay the responsibilities of biblical religion and place great stress on the freedom of Christianity. Christianity is about faith, not mindless obedience, goes the saying, and that's about all that needs to be said. Little wonder that so many professing Christians struggle to achieve a consistent life.

In the most ironic of ways, the good life, that which offers humanity boundless happiness, is actually the life of obedience, albeit joyful obedience. Those who end up the happiest in this life, the Bible teaches, are those whose hearts so boil over with love for the Lord that they cannot help but happily follow Him. One cannot read texts like Psalm 119 and claim that the Bible teaches anything but an inseparable connection between faith and holiness. "In the way of your testimonies I delight as much as in all riches," exclaims the Psalmist. "I will delight in your statutes; I will not forget your word" (Psalm 119:14, 16). The Scripture teaches in countless places the truth found in these exclamations of praise: The path to true joy is found in the contours of a life obedient to God's Word. Indeed, it is not in *leaving* the path laid out for us by God that we find satisfaction, but in *staying on it*, following the way of life designed by almighty God to bless us (see Proverbs 1 and 2, for example).

Jonathan Edwards knew this truth, and both lived it out and taught it. He had little time for religious moralists, and he had little time for selfish hedonists. He practiced, rather, a brand of faith that reflected the biblical reality that joy derives from obedience to God. Such a way of life was not natural, of course, after the fall; it was natural for mankind to stray from the righteous path and seek their fulfillment in sin. Although this deceptive train of thought ensnared many, Edwards knew that if he was to taste the goodness of God and the sweetness of Christ, he would need to conform his life to the will of God. The good life was the obedient life; the obedient life, conversely, was the good life.

In a number of Edwards's writings, he taught this biblical doctrine, injecting great passion and intellectual energy into it, trying with all his strength to turn people away from worldly promises of happiness that he knew would prove deeply unsatisfying and joyless. In "The Importance and Advantage of a Thorough Knowledge of Divine Truth," a section from the *Religious Affections*, and "The True Christian's Life a Journey Towards Heaven," the pastors shows us that God has given us His Word and His law not to bind us or rob us of joy, but to show us the shape of the good life and lead us into fullness of happiness.

The Long Perspective of Faith

In order to properly approach the Christian life, one had to view it from a long perspective. That is, Edwards believed that one needed to see one's existence in terms of eternity, and to factor one's daily choices into the life to come. In "The

True Christian's Life a Journey Towards Heaven," Edwards challenged his congregation to motivate themselves to holy living by thinking ahead to the end of their earthly days. Life, he contended, is a journey toward heaven for the Christian, and so:

WE OUGHT NOT TO BE CONTENT with this world, or so to set our hearts on any enjoyments we have here as to rest in them. No, we ought to seek a better happiness. If we are surrounded with many outward enjoyments and things are comfortable to us; if we are settled in families and have those friends and relatives that are very desirable; if we have companions whose society is delightful to us; if we have children that are pleasant and likely, and in whom we see many promising qualifications, and live by good neigh-bors, and have much of the respect of others, have a good name and are generally beloved where we are known, and have comfortable and pleasant accommodations: yet we ought not to take up our rest in these things. We should not be willing to have these things for our portion, but should seek happiness in another world. . . . We should choose to leave 'em all in God's due time, that we might go to heaven, and there have the enjoyment of God. (*Works* 17, 430)

The pastor's main point was that Christians need always to be ready to "choose to leave" the things of this world. The believer, unlike the lost person caught up in worldly pleasure, chases "a better happiness" located "in another world." Edwards did not debase this world or the things of it, but rather exhorted his people to set their affection on heaven and God such that the things of this world would pale in comparison.

Living for the Future

Once the people of God freed themselves up to appreciate the things of God, they would have a greater desire to live holy lives. Without what is sometimes called an eschatological viewpoint—that is, a viewpoint that sees one's life in light of eternity—Christians would often struggle to live differently from the world. In "The True Christian's Life a Journey Towards Heaven," Edwards called his people to holiness, but he did so while reminding his people of the outcome of holiness:

> WE OUGHT TO SEEK HEAVEN by traveling in the way that leads thither. The way that leads to heaven is a way of holiness; we should choose and desire to travel thither in this way, and in no other.
>
> We should part with all those sins, those carnal appetites, that are as weights that will tend to hinder us in our traveling towards heaven; Hebrews 12:1, "let us lay aside every

weight, and the sin that doth so easily beset us, and let us run with patience the race that is set before us." However pleasant any practice or the gratification of any appetite may be, we must lay it aside, cast it away, if it be any hindrance, any stumbling block, in the way to heaven.

All of the commands of God required the heaven-seeker's attention, according to the pastor:

WE SHOULD TRAVEL ON as a way of obedience to all God's commands, even the difficult, as well as the easy, commands. We should travel on in a way of self-denial, denying all our sinful inclinations and interests. The way to heaven is ascending; we must be content to travel up hill, though it be hard, and tiresome, and contrary to the natural tendency and bias of our flesh, that tends downward to the earth. We should follow Christ in the path that he has gone; the way that he traveled in was the right way to heaven. We should take up our cross and follow him. We should travel along in the same way of meekness and lowliness of heart, in the same way of obedience, and charity, and diligence to do good, and patience under afflictions. (*Works* 17, 433)

The good life, as we have frequently noted, is the best life, but it is not always, or even often, easy. One has to fight against the flesh, one's sinful nature, to acquire holiness and taste the sweetness of Christ. Christian faith, contrary to what some may tell us, is "a way of obedience" plotted according to "all God's commands," both the "difficult" and the "easy." It is "a way of self-denial." It is "ascending" and can be "hard, and tiresome." If we would walk it, and follow the example of the Savior, we must "take up our cross and follow him." The good life, the existence full of joy, does not involve self-exaltation, pride, and boastful celebration of one's strengths and talents, but "meekness," "lowliness of heart," "charity" for all, and "patience under afflictions." But we need not adopt these attitudes grimly. As our lives take a cruciform shape, godliness brings us joy, far more joy than sin does. But we must recognize as Edwards wisely does that obedience often involves hard work and vigilant concentration. We don't placate or pacify our flesh to grow in holiness; we fight it and kill it, doing war with it as we journey to our home above (Colossians 3:1–10).

Keeping Heaven Always in View

The good life is lived with heaven firmly in view. It is far off, yes, and sometimes difficult to see. But it is always in view. When one loses sight of heaven, one's faith cannot help but slip, one's resolve naturally begins to weaken. For this reason, one must always evaluate one's days according to a heavenward perspective. Our business decisions, our parenting, our classwork, our entertainment—we must consider all these things and many more from an eternal perspective. If we do not, as the pastor noted in "Journey Towards Heaven":

> ALL OUR LABOR WILL BE LOST. If we spend our lives in the pursuit of a temporal happiness; if we set our hearts on riches and seek happiness in them; if we seek to be happy in sensual pleasures; if we spend our lives to seek the credit and esteem of men, the good will and respect of others; if we set our hearts on our children and look to be happy in the enjoyment of them, in seeing them well brought up, and well settled, etc., all these things will be of little signif-icancy to us. Death will blow up all our hopes and expec-tations, and will put an end to our enjoyment of these things. . . . Where will be all our worldly employments and enjoyments when we are laid in the silent grave? For "man lieth down, and riseth not again: till the heavens be no more" (Job 14:12). (*Works* 17, 436–37)

Nothing temporal, however virtuous, would last in the end, not the finest "sensual pleasures," not the tenderest care for our children. "Death," the pastor boldly suggested, "will blow up all our hopes and expectations." Edwards left no doubt about the outcome of our worldly pursuits. The secular good life produces nothing but dust in the wind, embers of a fire now gone out. All one's "enjoyments" come to nothing. The wisdom of man, expressed in a thousand ways while living, crumbles "in the silent grave." Having ignored the wisdom of God all his life, the natural man follows his own wisdom to death.

The Benefits of Divine Wisdom

Edwards believed that God had designed His special creation, the human race, to do more than die an insignificant death. He had revealed Himself in the Bible so that sinners might abandon the broad way of destruction and find the narrow way of resurrection. In "The Importance and Advantage of a Thorough Knowledge of Divine Truth," Edwards discussed how the Bible manifested the treasures of God to the human race:

THESE THINGS ARE SO EXCELLENT and worthy to be known, that the knowledge of them will richly pay for all the pains and labor of an earnest seeking of it. If there were a great treasure of gold and pearls hid in the earth but should accidentally be found, and should be opened among us with such circumstances that all might have as much as they could gather of it; would not every one think it worth his while to make a business of gathering it while it should last? But that treasure of divine knowledge, which is contained in the Scriptures, and is provided for everyone to gather to himself as much of it as he can, is a far more rich treasure than any one of gold and pearls. How

busy are all sorts of men, all over the world, in getting
riches? But this knowledge is a far better kind of riches,
than that after which they so diligently and laboriously
pursue. (*Works* 22, 92)

Those who wanted to know true pleasure and lasting happiness, Edwards argued, needed to mine the Scripture, for in it
"is a far more rich treasure than any one of gold and pearls."
Everyone could obtain this treasure, Edwards noted, and the
delights of it would "richly pay for all the pains and labor of an
earnest seeking of it." Though some thought that following
the Bible would squelch happiness and rob people of pleasure, Edwards believed that it offered mankind the only sure
means to joy. God had made it plain and understandable, the
pastor contended, so that we could receive the benefits of the
good life. We must, then, seek them out with the same hunger
a treasure-hunter has for gold, or prospectors for oil:

WHEN GOD HATH OPENED a very large treasure before,
for the supply of our wants, and we thank him that he hath
given us so much; if at the same time we be willing to
remain destitute of the greatest part of it, because we are
too lazy to gather it, this will not show the sincerity of our
thankfulness. We are now under much greater advantages
to acquire knowledge in divinity, than the people of God
were of old; because since that time, the canon of Scripture
is much increased. But if we be negligent of our advantages,

we may be never the better for them, and may remain with
as little knowledge as they. (*Works* 22, 95)

Edwards admonished his people to direct their natural
appetites and energy to the Bible. He implored his fellow
Christians to realize the powers of their mind and to harness
these abilities to store up biblical knowledge that would fuel
holy living:

THIS KNOWLEDGE IS EXCEEDING useful in Christian
practice. Such as have much knowledge in divinity have
great means and advantages for spiritual and saving
knowledge; for no means of grace, as was said before, have
their saving effect on the heart, otherwise than by the
knowledge they impart. The more you have of a rational
knowledge of the things of the gospel, the more opportunity will there be, when the Spirit shall be breathed into
your heart, to see the excellency of these things, and to taste
the sweetness of then. The heathens, who have no rational
knowledge of the things of the gospel, have no opportunity to see the excellency of them; and therefore the more
rational knowledge of these things you have, the more
opportunity and advantage you have to see the divine
excellence and glory of them. (*Works* 22, 99–100)

Without the hard work of Scripture reading, meditation, and memorization, one would never see the "divine excellence and glory" of the Bible. Many Christians, Edwards knew, wanted to grow spiritually. They wanted to know God and go to heaven. But far fewer believers worked hard to deepen their faith and, subsequently, their enjoyment of God. Too many presumed upon God and His grace, expecting Him to simply drop a bag of maturity and happiness out of the sky for quick and easy use. This was not how Christian growth and maturity worked, the pastor argued. One had to apply one's mind, one's "rational knowledge," to "the things of the gospel." Only then could one see their "excellency" and taste their "sweetness." Christians have incredible "opportunity and advantage" to do so, with guaranteed results, but have to hungrily pursue such a life to experience it (Matthew 5:6).

Reframing Our Understanding of Scripture

Edwards's material reframes modern conceptions of the Scripture and its commands. As he understood it, the Bible is not merely a textbook or rulebook, but rather a living document that communicates the heart and mind of the Lord of the universe. It does not simply help us to sharpen and hone our lives or merely teach us content about God. The Bible opens to us the character of God. It presents God and the things of God to us. From every corner of the Bible we gain wisdom, instruction, encouragement, and an understanding of the magnificence and beauty of Christ. The stories of

Israelite heroes propel us to take heart in God and attempt great things for Him; the Law teaches us the inherent holiness of God and the required holiness of mankind; the Prophets show us the need to put holiness into practice; the Wisdom writings offer us a model for godly living and sage counsel for all seasons of life; the Gospels bring us face to face with Christ the Redeemer; the Epistles deliver grace-saturated teaching and exhortation; and Revelation shows us our future state in all its glory. All of Scripture is profitable for us, all of it will shape our lives in holy ways, all of it will quench our thirst and hunger for happiness through its exaltation of the Son, the Savior sent by the Father and empowered through the Spirit.

As we saturate our lives with the various texts of Scripture, we will experience an increasing closeness with God. He will become our joy and our hope. We will find assurance of our salvation, one of the most coveted and least-attained blessings in the Christian life. So many of us struggle in this area because our lives have not taken their shape from the Bible, and thus we lack assurance that we have been born again. We act and talk much like the lost around us. As a pastor who dealt his entire career with a worldly congregation (as many pastors do), Edwards fought to show his people that the turmoil and distress they experienced in their lives as a result of weak faith could cease. If they would pursue joy in Christ, and study the Word to find it, they would discover fresh assurance of their conversion, robbing Satan of one of his chief tools for undermining individual Christians and the broader ministry of the church.

In his classic text *The Religious Affections*, Edwards discussed this matter in a meaty section on the "twelfth sign of true Christian faith." There he defined godliness as "light that shines in the soul" and clarified the connection between words and deeds:

> AND AS THIS IS THE EVIDENCE that Christ has directed us mainly to look at in others, in judging of them, so it is the evidence that Christ has mainly directed us to give to others, whereby they may judge of us; "Let your light so shine before men, that others seeing your good works, may glorify your Father which is in heaven" (Matthew 5:16). Here Christ directs us to manifest our godliness to others. Godliness is as it were a light that shines in the soul: Christ directs that this light should not only shine within, but that it should shine out before men, that they may see it. But which way shall this be? 'Tis by our good works. Christ don't say, that others hearing your good words, your good story, or your pathetical expressions; but that others seeing your good works, may glorify your Father which is in heaven.

He continued:

> [T]HE APOSTLE [PAUL] in the beginning of the [sixth chapter of Hebrews], speaks of them that have great common illuminations, that have been enlightened, and have tasted

of the heavenly gift, and were made partakers of the Holy
Ghost, and have tasted the good Word of God, and the
powers of the world to come, that afterwards fall away, and
are like barren ground, that is nigh unto cursing, whose
end is to be burned: and then immediately adds in the 9th
verse (expressing his charity for the Christian Hebrews, as
having that saving grace, which is better than all these
common illuminations): "But beloved, we are persuaded
better things of you, and things that accompany salvation;
though we thus speak." And then in the next verse, he tells
'em what was the reason he had such good thoughts of
'em: he don't say, that it was because they had given him a
good account of a work of God upon their souls, and talked
very experimentally; but it was their work, and labor of
love; "For God is not unrighteous, to forget your work, and
labor of love, which ye have shewed towards his name, in
that ye have ministered to the saints, and do minister."
(*Works* 2, 407–8)

Having carefully spelled out how true faith manifests itself in
good works, Edwards then covered how an active faith, one
that conforms to the gracious contours of God's Word, produces assurance:

[T]HE SCRIPTURE ALSO SPEAKS of Christian practice as a
distinguishing and sure evidence of grace to persons' own

consciences. This is very plain in 1 John 2:3: "Hereby we do
know that we know him, if we keep his commandments."
And the testimony of our consciences, with respect to our
good deeds, is spoken of as that which may give us assurance of our own godliness; "My little children, let us not
love in word, neither in tongue, but in deed . . . and in
truth. And hereby we know that we are of the truth, and
shall assure our hearts before him" (1 John 3:18–19). And
the apostle Paul, in Hebrews 6 speaks of "the work and
labor of love," of the Christian Hebrews, as that which both
gave him a persuasion that they had something above the
highest common illuminations, and also as that evidence
which tended to give them the highest assurance of hope
concerning themselves; ver. Hebrews 6:9, etc.: "But beloved,
we are persuaded better things of you, and things that
accompany salvation, though we thus speak. For God is not
unrighteous, to forget your work, and labor of love, which
ye have showed towards his name; in that ye have ministered to his saints, and do minister. And we desire that
every one of you do show the same diligence, to the full
assurance of hope, unto the end." So the Apostle directs the
Galatians to examine their behavior or practice, that they
might have rejoicing in themselves in their own happy
state; "Let every man prove his own work; so shall he have

rejoicing in himself, and not in another" (Galatians 6:4).
(*Works* 2, 420–21)

In these selections, the pastor communicated principally that holy living produces assurance, and assurance produces joy. Life according to God's design, then, is not simply *right*, but is *rich*, full of the highest pleasure of the world, namely, happiness resulting from the favor of God. Contrary to how so many of us perceive self-examination, as a stringent, joyless, depression-inducing affair, Edwards teaches us that examining our lives will actually lead to "rejoicing" and leave us in a "happy state" due to an awareness of the love and good works the Spirit has worked within us. It will also give us fresh recognition of our sins and a renewed resolve to fight them.

The Need to Study Our Soul

As mentioned, however, most of us view self-examination as something negative. Because our feelings are sensitive and our hearts are proud, we hesitate to assess ourselves honestly. We do not want the floorboards of our hearts pulled up. Though it maims us, we want to keep our sin hidden. In reality, though, we are only hurting ourselves and those around us, because we are allowing sin to rule us. Self-examination, then, is a crucial practice, for it brings our sin to light and allows grace to shine in our hearts and uncover what we've buried. Our duty, then, is to make our conscience our friend, to listen to it as a trusted confidant, knowing that if it is submitted to God, it will guide us on the right path, and give us happy assurance in Christ.

Tracing the Good Life

The good life had a definite shape, as Edwards showed throughout his writings. God did not create us, save us, and then leave us to do whatever we wished. He gave us a way of holiness to follow. He gave us a Bible with teaching to guide us. He gave us a conscience to lead us to holiness despite the presence of sin in our hearts. In all of these ways, God has given the good life a certain form, a definite shape, that He desires all His children to emulate. Edwards repeatedly emphasized, though, that this way of life did not squelch true joy—it produced it. It did squelch a certain kind of pleasure, a worldly, narcissistic, law-breaking pleasure, but it produced a better, lasting delight. True freedom and joy did not for Edwards proceed from egoistic hedonism, as our culture tells us, but from freeing obedience to the dictates of Scripture and the direction of God's Spirit.

Edwards showed throughout his writings on the good life that God originally made His people to walk in perfect harmony with Him. Even before the fall of Adam and Eve, this involved living according to His commands and laws. Restored humanity, those who had been regenerated by the Spirit, once again walked with God in harmony, enabled by the Spirit to experience the bliss of obedience. Freed from the power of sin, the children of God tasted all kinds of blessings—divine love, peace, hope, confidence, endurance, comfort, power, and more. They benefited from the guidance of the Word and experienced, as they repented daily of sin, the ongoing pleasantness of a clean conscience.

Edwards proved that the Lord was not harsh to give us direction in His word, but kind. God desired that we experience delight all of our days and graciously created the ideal conditions for a delightful life, which we have called the good life. This life does not run contrary to our best interests, but serves them even as it fulfills the good purposes of the Lord for our lives. It frees us from slavery to our lower, natural appetites and passions incurred by original sin and enables higher, spiritual principles to lead us. It turns us away from self-driven destruction and places us on a holy journey that is sometimes quite challenging but rewarding both here and in the afterlife. This, and not any other version, is the good life, the life God intends for us.

Living the Good Life

Honor the Lord through Sincere, Passionate Obedience

*O*urs is not an age that prizes obedience. We have grown up in an anti-authoritarian culture in which the watchword is something like "Do what pleases you and don't judge others." Some Christians have imbibed this spirit as well and seem to think that their faith has no room for God's laws, commandments, or directions for living.

This mindset, which emphasizes faith and the heart over obedience and the mind, alters the biblical picture of the Christian life. In true biblical religion, heart and mind go together and faith fuels obedience. Past generations of Christians have, it is true, gone overboard with rules and laws and have sometimes seemed to reduce the robust life offered us in the gospel to a set of commands. We should reject such a mindset—though we should also remember that the Bible includes many commands and guidelines for the believer to follow.

Once the Holy Spirit converts our fallen hearts, we are called to devote ourselves to lives of holiness and obedience. This does not mean that we cannot also pursue joy. As we have seen in Edwards's writings, we must pursue joy, and in fact, we will find the fullness of joy when our hearts seek to worship the Lord in what the Apostle Paul called "the obedi-ence of faith" (Romans 1:5, 16:26). Thus, we should never divide holiness from happiness. We must not let the culture determine our understanding of God's character and His law. His law, after all, is not some arbitrary code of conduct, but is both the expression of His character and His beneficent will for mankind.

As with so many other points of application, we need churches that prioritize holiness to encourage us in this direc-tion; we need close friends who keep us accountable and push us on to good works; and we need a close personal walk with the Lord that will allow us to cultivate a rich, happy, holy walk with God. The difference between formalized Christianity, Christianity that looks fine but really is just an exercise to per-form without any real passion, and the good life can boil down to sincerity and passion. If we would taste the goodness of God, then we need to sincerely, not half-heartedly, pursue the Lord. This means that we don't simply pray to do it; that we don't just read the sacred text; that we don't simply show up to church, but that we do all these out of a sincere, earnest, passionate desire to love the Lord. The world mocks sincerity, but it is inseparable from true faith and the good life.

Seek Assurance through Godliness

*I*n our day, we often hear statements like, "Well, I'm a believer, but I'm not really into religion." "I love Jesus, but I don't believe in all these rules." "Yeah, I trust God, but the whole church thing gets way overblown." In these and many other such statements, people with a lax faith excuse themselves from true Christian living. This is a tragedy. They may have a basic belief in God, but without salvation, and thus be tricking themselves into thinking they are eternally secure when they are not. Or, they may truly be saved, but dishonoring the Lord through a half-hearted, passionless, unholy lifestyle.

True believers in this situation, as with all of us who profess Christ, need to act upon the Edwardsean idea that godliness will generally provide clarity and assurance of our faith (see 1 John 5, for example). Those who constantly doubt their Christian profession need to know that only a godly life, coupled with the witness of the Holy Spirit and the encouragement of a church, will produce true confidence in Christ. None of us will obtain perfection (or anything close to it) until heaven, but the Lord has designed our faith to gain rich assurance when it is driven by an obedient, God-centered heart.

The Good Life Examined

*W*e have now explored what the good life truly is. It is not a matter of personal gratification; it is not an exercise in narcissistic self-love. It is a transformative journey from death to life, a journey toward transcendence begun when the Holy Spirit brings a cold heart to feel the warmth of Christ's fiery love. This action restores the heart and will of man, returning each to its original purpose and design, causing showers of blessing to pour into the regenerate soul. The good life, we have noted, has definite shape and form, and cannot be programmed however one sees fit. God has created this way of existence, and God directs it. Far from being an impediment to happiness, however, this simple fact assures us with the strongest confidence that the good life of the Bible, unlike all other versions, is the only life worth living.

The good life alone, in contrast with all other contenders for this title, elevates the soul beyond this world. No other existence leads us to heaven, where we will truly see God face to face, and worship Him forever. In words both plain and stirring, Jonathan Edwards captured this reality in "The True Christian's Life a Journey Towards Heaven." There he reminded his flock, so weighed down with the cares and trials of this world, that:

> THE WAY TO HEAVEN is an heavenly life. We must be trav-eling towards heaven in a way of imitation of those that are in heaven, in imitation of the saints or angels therein, in their holy employments, in their way of spending their time in loving, adoring, serving, and praising God and the Lamb.
>
> This is the path that we prefer before all others. If we could have any other that we might choose, if we could go to heaven in a way of carnal living, the way of the enjoy-ment and gratification of our lusts, we should rather prefer a way of holiness, and conformity to the spiritual, self-denying rules of the gospel. (*Works* 17, 433)

May we believe these words, and follow the path of the good life until all our "traveling" ceases and we enter the eternal home God has prepared for us—and for which we have been prepared.

Acknowledgments

*W*e have a number of people to thank for the production of this volume.

We would like to thank Dave DeWit of Moody Publishers. Dave is an excellent editor and has been a tremendous help and encouragement in all aspects of the process. It was Dave who suggested that this project encompass not one book, but five, forming a comprehensive and definitive introductory series. We are thankful for his vision. We would also thank Chris Reese, who gave excellent feedback on this and every manuscript and made each book clearer and better.

We would like to thank Dr. John Piper for graciously providing a series foreword. It is a signal honor to have Dr. Piper involved in this project. Dr. Piper has enriched our understanding of Jonathan Edwards as he has for countless people. We are thankful to the Lord for his ministry, and we deeply appreciate his commendation of this collection. We are thankful as well for the assistance of David Mathis, Executive Pastoral Assistant to Dr. Piper.

We would like to thank close friends who gave encouragement at various points in the project. To Jed Atkins, Colin LeCroy, Suen Wong, and Ralph Knowles—thank you.

Owen dedicates this book to his treasured friend Keegan, for his enduring friendship, excellent counsel, and Christlike example.

Doug dedicates this book to his wife, Wilma Sweeney, from whom he's learned so very much about the good life.

Above all others, we thank our great God, the One whose goodness flows from heaven into our lives here.

Recommended Resources on
Jonathan Edwards

*F*or the premier collection of Edwards's own writings, see
The Works of Jonathan Edwards, vol. 1–26, Yale University Press. Access these works in their entirety free of charge
at http://edwards.yale.edu.

For secondary sources, we recommend the following.

Introductory Reading

Byrd, James P. *Jonathan Edwards for Armchair Theologians.*
   Louisville, KY: Westminster John Knox Press, 2008.
McDermott, Gerald R. *Seeing God: Jonathan Edwards and
   Spiritual Discernment.* Vancouver: Regent College Pub-
   lishing, 2000.

Nichols, Stephen A. *Jonathan Edwards: A Guided Tour of His Life and Thought.* Phillipsburg, NJ: Presbyterian & Reformed, 2001.

Storms, Sam. *Signs of the Spirit: An Interpretation of Jonathan Edwards' Religious Affections.* Wheaton, IL: Crossway Books, 2007.

Deeper Reading

Gura, Philip F. *Jonathan Edwards: America's Evangelical.* New York: Hill & Wang, 2005.

Kimnach, Wilson H., Kenneth P. Minkema, and Douglas A. Sweeney, eds. *The Sermons of Jonathan Edwards: A Reader.* New Haven: Yale University Press, 1999.

Lesser, M. X. *Reading Jonathan Edwards: An Annotated Bibliography in Three Parts, 1729–2005.* Grand Rapids: Eerdmans, 2008

Marsden, George. *Jonathan Edwards: A Life.* New Haven: Yale University Press, 2003.

McDermott, Gerald R., ed. *Understanding Jonathan Edwards: An Introduction to America's Theologian.* New York: Oxford University Press, 2009.

Moody, Josh. *The God-Centered Life: Insights from Jonathan Edwards for Today.* Vancouver: Regent College Publishing, 2007.

Murray, Iain H. *Jonathan Edwards: A New Biography.* Edinburgh: Banner of Truth Trust, 1987.

Piper, John. *God's Passion for His Glory: Living the Vision of Jonathan Edwards.* Wheaton, IL: Crossway Books, 1998.

———, and Justin Taylor, eds. *A God Entranced Vision of All Things: The Legacy of Jonathan Edwards.* Wheaton, IL: Crossway Books, 2004.

Smith, John E., Harry S. Stout, and Kenneth P. Minkema, eds. *A Jonathan Edwards Reader.* New Haven: Yale University Press, 1995.

Sweeney, Douglas A. *Jonathan Edwards and the Ministry of the Word: A Model of Faith and Thought.* Downers Grove, IL: InterVarsity Press, 2009.

BRINGING YOU THE TIMELESS CLASSICS

Classics

Selected for their enduring influence and timeless perspective ...

Answers to Prayer
ISBN-13: 978-0-8024-5650-2

The Confessions
of St. Augustine
ISBN-13: 978-0-8024-5651-9

How to Pray
ISBN-13: 978-0-8024-5652-6

The Imitation of Christ
ISBN-13: 978-0-8024-5653-3

The Pilgrim's Progress
ISBN-13: 978-0-8024-5654-0

The True Vine
ISBN-13: 978-0-8024-5655-7

Power Through Prayer
ISBN-13: 978-0-8024-5662-5

The Christian's Secret
of a Happy Life
ISBN-13: 978-0-8024-5656-4

Hudson Taylor's
Spiritual Secret
ISBN-13: 978-0-8024-5658-8

MOODY
PUBLISHERS
MoodyClassics.com

BRINGING YOU THE TIMELESS CLASSICS

Classics

... these are key books that every believer on the journey of spiritual formation should read.

Holiness
ISBN-13: 978-0-8024-5455-3

Born Crucified
ISBN-13: 978-0-8024-5456-0

Names of God
ISBN-13: 978-0-8024-5856-8

The Overcoming Life
ISBN-13: 978-0-8024-5451-5

All of Grace
ISBN-13: 978-0-8024-5452-2

The Secret
of Guidance
ISBN-13: 978-0-8024-5454-6

The Incomparable Christ
ISBN-13: 978-0-8024-5660-1

Orthodoxy
ISBN-13: 978-0-8024-5657-1

The Apostolic Fathers
ISBN-13: 978-0-8024-5659-5

MOODY
PUBLISHERS
MoodyClassics.com